# AWAKENING

# AWAKENING

## LIFE AND TIMES OF

## EAMONN COTTER

Tandy Publications

First published in Republic of Ireland in 2000 by

Tandy Publications,
47 Westbury Drive, Lucan, Co. Dublin.
Email: freamonn@indigo.ie

© Eamonn Cotter, 2000

ISBN   0-9539093-0-1

The right of Eamonn Cotter to be identified as the author of this work has been asserted by him in accordance with the Copyright, Designs and Patents Act 1988.

All rights reserved. No part of this publication may be reproduced, stored in a retrieval system, or transmitted in any form or by any means, electronic, mechanical, photocopying, recording, or otherwise, without the prior permission in writing of the publisher.

"On the sands of hesitation bleach the bones of those, who close to victory, stopped to rest, and in resting, died."

# ACKNOWLEDGEMENTS

It would be impossible to produce a book like this, especially for one making the first attempt, without help and encouragement from a number of people. A few names of such people must be mentioned: Jack Harte, Pat O'Brien, Gerry Tanham, Helen Brannick, Glen O'Toole.

Jacinta Cotter (Front cover art work)

For her tireless editorial work on the book, and being the instigator of the idea in the first place, this volume would not have been produced without the many months of extremely hard work by Catherine Cotter.

# DEDICATION

*IN GRATITUDE TO THE GOOD LORD FOR FAVOURS RECEIVED, I DEDICATE THIS LITTLE BOOK TO MY LOVING, FAMILY, LIVING AND DEAD.*

# CONTENTS

|    | Foreword | 1 |
|----|----------|---|
|    | Introduction | 3 |
| 1  | Home and School - Part One | 5 |
| 2  | Home and School - Part Two | 40 |
| 3  | Future Taking Shape | 68 |
| 4  | Appointments | 89 |
|    | *Ravenswell Convent and School* | |
|    | *Ranelagh* | |
|    | *St. Michael's Hospital, Dun Laoghaire* | |
| 5  | London Hotel Chaplaincy | 100 |
| 6  | Hobbies and Pastimes | 129 |
| 7  | The "All Priests Show" and me | 136 |
| 8  | Appointments | 146 |
|    | *Rathcoole* | |
|    | *The Navan Road* | |
|    | *Kilcoole* | |
|    | *Esker-Lucan* | |
| 9  | Struggle with Alcohol | 173 |
| 10 | Bereavements | 197 |
| 11 | The Church. Yesterday-Today-Tomorrow | 202 |

# FOREWORD

In sharing his life-story with us Eamonn Cotter has achieved many things at once. He has provided us with a very interesting, very readable, and very entertaining biography. He has also provided us with an extremely important social document. The account of his days as a student for the priesthood and as a young priest in the 1950's and 1960's is quite remarkable in its frank honesty as well as its familiar detail. It will be a revelation to many readers to find that those hey-days of Church power and status were not so kind as one would imagine to the young priest. Eamonn's uncompromising narrative of his experience of ministry in the Church of Archbishop McQuaid is an extremely valuable insight into a very important aspect of the social history of that time.

Eamonn Cotter was born into a large family, typical of the time, and the way in which his relationship with his family changed and evolved is also fascinating. The Church and priests have been the subject of criticism, indignation and condemnation in recent years, and perhaps it is now time to give some consideration to the struggling human beings who constitute the Church and the Priesthood. Eamonn's book provides an account of such a struggling human being with heart-rending honesty. His specific struggle with alcoholism is dealt with in an absolutely forth-right manner, showing that the priest has his demons like everyone else. It is a measure of Eamonn's success, his nobility, and his deep humanity, that after much pain he has established equilibrium in his own life and has the moral courage to share his experiences with the rest of us. In doing so he displays the natural flair of the story-teller, entertaining us even as he is enlightening us.

*Jack Harte*

# INTRODUCTION

This book came about as a result of the constructive suggestion and invitation of my niece Catherine, and so I set out on this journey of writing about my life and times. Having over the years journeyed to most of the big, and often dreamed of, cities and countries of the world, through the medium of show business, golf, holidays and the like, I never really seriously undertook in a formulated manner, the journey of my own personal life, the journey of reality, and the journey with people and God.

The challenge of writing a book had never entered my mind over the years. I also felt quite elated with the idea that I had a story that might be worth telling and perhaps others might enjoy. At the same time I knew that the whole exercise would be most therapeutic in the area of my own personal well being and recovery.

The suggestion of writing this volume was first made to me in February of the New Millennium, and work began in March of the same year. As the work progressed I realized that my memory was serving me well, and I was quite happy with what was a emerging. I felt a great sense of personal freedom and control in presenting an honest, open and down to earth "real life" account of my time in this world so far. For me this piece of work has been a liberating experience. Hopefully it will be enlightening, entertaining, uplifting and perhaps even moving and helpful to some readers.

I feel in my heart now that this book was meant to be written. As I to put ink to paper, with a rather winding chronological sequence of events in my life's journey, I'll endeavour to bring you, the reader, with me into all the wider as well as the more personal happenings along the way and in a very simple presentation perhaps give some insight into one who enjoys the simple things in life and loves people.

# CHAPTER ONE

## HOME AND SCHOOL - PART I

***Birth date and era.***
I was the sixth of ten children born on April 4$^{th}$ 1938 into a small thirty acre Land Commission farm which had been part of the greater holding of St.Wolstans. It was about a mile from Celbridge on the Dublin Rd., but well within the Kildare boundaries and therefore I qualified fully to be called a "Lilly White."
Little did I know that 1938 was the eve of world war two and in that year Franco's forces divided the republicans of Spain in two. In London, people were being measured for gas masks. Key Jewish figures from Vienna were being sent to Dachau concentration camp. In Dublin, Douglas Hyde was elected Ireland's first President. Some names of world leaders in that year were: Neville Chamberlain (U.K.), Franklin Roosevelt (U.S.), Joseph Stalin (Russia) and in Ireland we had Eamon deValera. The Pope at the time was Pius X1.
There are always happenings very early in any person's life that can only be told by other people simply because we don't remember, we were too young. Some of the memories that certain people love to remind us of are ones we would rather forget. There are a couple of these I'm never allowed to forget. The bigger brothers of course were always great fellas for getting the boot in and asking things like, "Do you remember the day you got the needle up your bum?" How could I.? I was one year old and the baby in arms at the time.

Apparently, my mother was doing some knitting while holding me in her arms. She was called suddenly to give her immediate attention to something else and being in a bedroom, she literally threw me on the nearby bed on which there was a bundle of wool and other knitwear, not knowing that there was a large darning needle sticking up somewhere in the middle of everything on the bed. The needle went deep into my posterior and in the course of the many reminders I got over the years, the more polite ones used the word bum, but in latter years I have been asked, "Do you remember when you got the needle up your arse?" I'm glad I was too young when it happened to have a vivid memory of that experience.

For some years I was the first to be packed off to bed and I'm regularly reminded of a night when my parents and some older members of the family had a few rather important visitors in the sitting room and we had to pass through this sitting room to get to any other room in the house. I appeared into the middle of this gathering in the nip, with no inhibitions whatsoever and I just proceeded to ask for what I wanted. I'm glad I don't remember that one either. We shared beds in the early years and once one left the warmth of the room where the fire was going, the only other warm and best place to be was in bed. Everything was simple and basic in clothing, food and house-life, but we had what we needed and I don't ever remember being extremely cold or hungry and if any of us needed support and comfort, that was to be found in the parents or the older members of the family.

**Earliest memories.**
If I was to try and describe the sequence of a life's story, it could not be summed up better than it is in the Book of Ecclesiastes Ch. 3. "There is a reason for everything, a time for every occupation under Heaven: A time for giving birth, a time for dying; a time for planting, a time for uprooting what has been planted; a time for killing, a time for healing; a time for knocking down, a time for building; a time for tears, a time

for laughter; a time for mourning, a time for dancing; a time for throwing stones away, a time for gathering them up; a time for embracing, a time for refraining from embracing; a time for searching, a time for losing; a time for keeping, a time for throwing away; a time for tearing, a time for sowing; a time for keeping silent, a time for speaking; a time for loving, a time for hating; a time for war, a time for peace."

People often say that there is a time, a place and a reason for everything that happens to us in life. Sometimes we wonder at this when we find ourselves in unusual and difficult circumstances and it's only looking back over life that one can appreciate in a more objective way what has really taken place. Where one has faith in a power higher than ourselves, viz. God, then that helps and supports.

My earliest memories go back to four years of age and some of them are as clear and realistic today as they were then, especially the most frightening and enjoyable ones. At the age of four, I was no longer the baby, as I now had two younger brothers, the younger being the baby in arms. With eight now in the family, I was the senior of the last trio and like the small nervous animal emerging for the first time from its den to look at the big wide world outside, I ventured one day down the farm yard to witness what was a major undertaking for my father and older brothers. It was the killing of some pigs, after which the meat would be salted and put hanging in the pantry or some cool spot, as provisions for the coming winter. I had been told by my father not to come down the yard because I was too young and as I slowly sneaked from the door, my mother, who was sitting just inside at the sowing machine working away, said "You were told by your father not to go down there." Despite all the warnings and orders, I still had to see for myself what was going on. I took up my position at the corner from where I could see the large wooden bench on which the slaughtering was to happen and with that I heard the awful screeching of the pig. The first to appear was my father wielding a big knife and then it needed all three of the older brothers to hold down this kicking, struggling and desperate pig which I think sensed what was about to happen. At that stage I should really have left because that scene alone was enough to frighten the life out of me. But no, realizing I wasn't spotted by any of the very busy team, I had a clear view of the animal being unceremoniously planked on the bench and the knife being immediately plunged at its throat followed by a gush of blood as if from flood gates. The pig was then hoisted by its back legs to a waiting makeshift scaffold poll and the entire tummy was opened from which fell out all the entrails. With my mouth opened in shock, and holding my tummy in fear, I ran back to the door from which I had emerged. Like a chicken dashing under the mother hen, I ran to hide under my mother's apron and skirt. I could feel my mothers legs working away at the machine without any interruption in her rhythm, and not being in the least surprised by my sudden return and dash for cover and shelter. The only words she said were "You were told not to go out there, serves ya right." So you can understand why to this day I have never really liked any sort of bacon.

Soon I picked up courage and ventured again to explore the little farm yard making sure there were no screaming pigs about. There were lots of other animals I had yet to meet. I always loved animals and plants. There were about ten cows, a donkey, two horses, twenty laying hens, six or seven turkeys (all black) and a big turkey cock plus some geese and ducks. I was now four and a half years of age and quite grown up enough to make my presence felt around the yard. The first to attract my attention were the turkeys and I was fascinated with the big red face on the turkey cock. I studied how he fanned his tail like a peacock but he was not at all happy with me being around and he would come at me with his chin and head backed into his neck. He had a long skinny piece of flesh for a nose and of course his tail was fully fanned while moving from side to side. One day I found myself cornered in the yard with this "monster" coming at me. Like the pig, I was now screaming, but I must have been louder. My Father appeared from nowhere with his collar-less open necked shirt, sleeves rolled up and a big sun hat tilted back on his head, and I thought to myself, "great I'm rescued, I won't be gobbled up after all." But to my surprise and horror, he threw me a piece of stick and said, "Now, you got yourself in there, let me see you get yourself out." He just stood there with his arms folded and never did a thing to make the turkey cock back off. He didn't have to tell me what the stick was for. I bashed at its head, frantically swinging the stick back and forth, still screaming and shouting with tears flowing down my cheeks, until eventually, he withdrew and I was free. The minute it lasted seemed like an hour. My father just went on his way, remarking, "You won't annoy the turkeys in future." Gathering myself and not wishing to go back into my mother crying, I went over to the animal I grew to love dearly, our sheep dog named Shep.

On this occasion I was seeking some comfort after my awful experience with the turkey cock. I sat down beside him and he wagged his tail. He was a wonder dog and I really thought he understood what people said to him. I would hear my father simply say, "Shep, go get the cows," and off he'd go on his own up to the top field. We had three fields, the near, the middle and the top. From the yard we could see the cows and the donkey with them, all following their usual track in no big hurry as they were bursting with milk and some were expecting their little calves. Shep would doddle behind, flipping from side to side, having an odd look to make sure all his charges were moving along nicely. Each cow would then make her way without any fuss to her own stall to be milked. This was the most important chore of the day and only the experts knew how to milk a cow. I could never get the hang of it, no matter how hard I tried. I remember wondering to myself at this time, how was I going to fit into all of this and what my tasks and chores would be.

Whenever possible our main meal was eaten in the middle of the day, so the running order was breakfast, dinner and tea which was eaten about seven. However that became different for the school-going members. In the evening everything and everyone began to settle down, jostling around on the floor, trying to get near the fire if it was a cold night. Later in the evening everyone would kneel down for prayers. My father in his usual corner knelt to the left of the fire, my mother knelt on the other side, each at their chairs fingering their beads. To me what seemed like mumbo jumbo went on for ages and I was, as the kids often say today, "bored." I learned in time that this was "The Rosary." After what seemed like an eternity, each had to say their own night prayers out loud and as I was still learning I repeated some words after my mother which was my first introduction to a person called God. While we were at this my father would be tucking into a big plate of porridge with a bowl of milk on the side. The whole Family was firmly and very carefully made to realize that prayer and God were of the utmost importance. It was something sacred and I noticed that people's voices and manner changed somewhat when they were at these prayers.

Just as I was beginning school at about the age of five with the Holy Faith Sisters in Celbridge, the ninth member was added to the family and this time it was a girl. When I was somewhat settled at school, the tenth and final member of the family was about to descend on the house. Just as the previous two had been born away from home i.e. in a hospital, so too was the last. All the others were born at home, with the assistance of the midwife. The big taxi brought my mother away once again, and a few days later, we were told she was now on her way home and to the assembled family my father announced "You all have a new brother." I was genuinely waiting for a little guy to come running in kicking a football. Instead my mother arrived with a screaming little bundle wrapped up out of sight and when I did get a look at him I could only see a smudgy little face, with a baldly head. He was immediately nick-named, "The Chief."

### *Family nicknames*
It was the custom in most families at that time to apply nicknames to one another and ours was no exception. As the youngest is already named above, I'll go from there to myself. I was nicknamed "Demo" because I was forever demonstrating and gesticulating with my hands as my way of conveying an idea, thought or story. The other nick names were "Schrone," "Winks," "Nibbler," "Redzer," "Crotts," "L," "Snotts," and "Drew." Most nicknames were imposed for a variety of reasons, mostly uncomplimentary. Very often they would arise out of an argument as an angry reaction to some upset. It could be the result of jealousy, revenge or vindictiveness. Sometimes the name emerged as a result of one's appearance, defect in character, or some idiosyncrasy. Nicknames initially were meant to hurt the other person and were often used in a bullying situation. For a combination of these reasons, the so-called nicknames came about in our family.

This all happened while we were quite young and each name was carefully selected in the shape of a curt and singular word with a meaning for the user and recipient. Some names were slow in emerging, as they had to be shaped, moulded, discussed, matured, experimented with, until eventually the final decision was made and the name then lasted a lifetime. Only in later years could members of the family laugh about all this in good fun.

### *Santa Claus*
When I was about three years old a most important mysterious character came into my life. At first I only heard stories about him. He was described as an old man with long white hair and beard, wearing a loose flowing red outfit with gloves and big boots. I was told that he arrived in the middle of winter from a distant country on a sleigh drawn by four deer, at a very

special time of the year called Christmas. He brought presents for all children, but only to those who were good and obedient. We were told that he came down the chimney in the middle of the night when all were asleep, especially the children for whom he had presents and if they were awake or made any attempt to have a look at him, they got nothing then or ever again. He loved some currant cake, milk and sometimes if it was available a bottle of stout. The manner in which all this was presented was most convincing, and I can recall the very first memory of waking up to my first visit from the man I came to know as Santa Claus.

My younger brother and I were sharing a bed and he too was aware of the big morning ahead. We awoke together at 5am and looked down at the foot of the bed and there for each of us were two identical little snow houses which were in fact two shoe boxes shaped into a house with doors and windows painted on and cotton wool on top for snow. As we grabbed the two special presents left by our "mysterious visitor" our first reaction was to shake them. Moving in harmony, we both realized there was something inside because there was a loud rattle and heavy thudding as we did our shaking. Together we ripped open our "snow houses" to discover an apple in each of them and we sat on the bed and began to eat. As this was the sum total of what we got from Santa, simple and small though it was, we were fully satisfied. The excitement was such that we had to share it immediately with someone and who better than our parents. We made a loud entrance into their bedroom with our torn snow house in one hand and a half eaten apple in the other, shouting, "Look at what we got from Santa and an apple as well." It was to be some years later before I realized how much work and care my father had put into making the little snow houses but at the time he could only join in sharing our joy and excitement.

**Formative years**

Without going into a deep study of one's formative years, it's generally accepted that one's very early days at home and in school constitute what any person is made of and grows up to be. Some say it begins from the cradle and all that follows is mere padding. There is no doubt that parents and other family members, the inherited genes, the personality traits that are learnt in childhood, must leave a lasting impression on a person's whole life. In my case, I can certainly look back on parents, home and family as the basic foundation of the person I have become. Every individual is different, even within the same family, and while there may be many characteristics that identify one with a particular family, there is always that personal individuality that makes each and every one of us unique. When I had to fight my way out of the corner from the attacking turkey cock, little did I think that that was a lesson in courage and part of my formation for life. That and many many other happenings which seemed insignificant at the time, were an invaluable and integral part of one's growing up to become the person with a mind and heart and body that was to survive by learning to battle on in life every step of the way. In my own case, home was for me the greatest and most effective part of my education.

My first day at school was a tearing away from that home and family where I really wanted to stay. But many had gone before me from the same secure and happy environment and being sixth in line, all my seniors were now well established at school. It was the law, my father told me, and if I didn't go I could have the local Garda Siochana come and take me away. A few such "musts" tossed at me, soon made me realize that my disapproval of school would be of no use and would get me nowhere. It was in such a frame of mind that I reluctantly began school. What followed did not in anyway help alleviate my apprehensions but in fact created only fear and sometimes even horror. Although I did wish to learn and I began to accept and understand the absolute necessity for school, I could not but feel that the system was at that time a force-feeding process, that was to leave me only with hatred for school. As my schooling years went on that same sort of system persisted right through and the deep dislike for school stayed with me all the way. The infant, primary and secondary school system involved beating the knowledge into the pupil. It is so different today, where teachers in a most professional manner, extract from the children the huge mountain of material which they have in a real sense built into them.

We walked one mile in our weekday clothes and in bare feet to school with a small lunch which consisted of two slices of bread with butter and jam and a small bottle of milk usually in a used mineral bottle. One morning at a spot about one third of the way, I was set upon by four other lads not much older than myself and while two of them held me against a wall, the other two gave me a good hiding. I gave them no reason for this, nor did I provoke them in anyway. I put it down to the fact that I was new. A certain gang had to show me and others who was really in charge and I had learned that I had to toughen up if I was to be an integral part of this group walking to school. You could call it a sort of initiation ceremony. I was bleeding and crying, sore and upset as I walked the rest of the way but I pulled myself together sufficiently for no one to notice anything when I got there. I felt anyway that I was being observed, and I wasn't going to let what was in fact my first experience of bullying get to me. I had my mind firmly made up not to mention a word to anyone at home and never did to this very day. But within the school itself I remember so well an unbelievable experience when a certain nun teacher pinned a clothes peg on to my tongue and made me stand with this hanging from my mouth in the corner for a half an hour, simply because I was talking in class. When I tell that story to people today, some smart ones from whom I would have expected sympathy, would say, "Well it didn't cure you." One of my older brothers got a crack of a black-thorn stick across the back once, leaving a huge bruise. We both reported these incidents at home and had the scars to prove it, but neither of us got any sympathy whatsoever, and in fact were told by the parents that we must have deserved it and the teacher could not be wrong. That was the end of that, what could we do?

I liked learning to write and read because I knew from the beginning this was the way for communicating with people and the world. I had no idea where it was all leading to but I knuckled down to retaining whatever I could. I was of average intelligence and had difficulty in remembering the many things we had to learn by heart. It was by sheer repetition that I managed to reach the required gradings.

Soon I was in first class and that meant preparing for confession and first Holy Communion. In practice, the nun would sit in where the priest should be and put us all through the routine many times, until it became second nature to us. I never repeated so many "sins" so many times, it should have done me for the rest of my life. Anyway the nun by this time knew all our "sins" off by heart and I often wondered how she could store them all or what she would do with them in the end. When it came to religion, the nuns were very thorough. We were told that our souls were cleansed from our dirty sins by confession, and for many years I thought my soul was the inside of the main torso of my body and I often looked for a glow of cleanliness every time I came out from confession. In later years a Dublin priest told me a story of when every month the children from the local school would all be marched to the church for confession and many priests would have to sit for hours and listen to much repetition. He told me how on one occasion an entire class seemed to have a very similar story. One after the other they would say, "I told lies, I was disobedient, I took sweets and I threw wee wee in the river." This identical routine came from dozens of boys and all finished with the same admission, "I threw wee wee in the river." So much so that while listening to yet one more of the same, the priest interrupted him in the middle and said, "And I suppose you threw wee wee in the river as well?" but the boy said, "No Father, I am wee wee."

### *First Holy Communion*

First Holy Communion was an outstanding and very happy memory for me. The nuns did a great job in preparation and there was an unforgettable build-up to the occasion. It was boys and girls mixed as were all the classes in the school at this junior stage. The style was great then as it is today and this meant I wore a lovely new suit and of course a big Holy Communion badge. There was a large turn out of people to the parish church on the day and it was very special for the entire community. There was also a family preparation and the input there would have been most sincere and genuine and everyone's attention was given to the one who was preparing for the big day .

The Mass was all in Latin and but for a few simple prayers towards the end in English which we repeated after the priest, the rest of the ceremony was above my head. But I did have a simple child-like belief and acceptance that something very special was happening that day and that Jesus was coming to me in the little host that we were receiving. There was no small anxiety when the host was placed on the tongue as we had been strictly warned not to let it even touch our teeth. This took a very delicate and careful manoeuvering with the tongue and there were lots of funny strained faces around in the church while this serious operation was going on. To chew the host or worse still to put your finger near it to help release it from the roof of the mouth, was unthinkable, and this was so instilled into us, that I thought, the whole world would fall down around us, such would be the calamity. Somehow, we got there and then it was time for the big march down the aisle, boy and girl side by side. I really felt proud making that walk and remembered it as my first real public appearance. In later life when I looked back on it, it was the only occasion I had the pleasure of walking a girl down the aisle!

The nuns put on a fabulous party in the school for everyone which was all over in about forty five minutes and that was it.

There was no family do at home or anywhere else. There was an older brother waiting to take me home, walking. Everyone else had gone and life at home resumed its usual routine for the remainder of that day. I was allowed to stay in my new suit because some relatives and friends were calling to see me and my father had given me a little wink earlier about this when he said "you might get a few bob from one or two of them." By the end of the day I had seven shillings in my pocket which I thought was an absolute fortune. But as you can guess I wasn't allowed to spend it as I would have liked. It was carefully put away for me to buy books and other things I would need for school. I really felt great on Sundays, as now I could join the others going to Mass and go to the altar with them to receive this special host which was Jesus in Holy Communion. As I was coming towards the end of first class, I knew by then that I was not going on to the local boys school as was the usual procedure. My two eldest brothers had gone there, it was called the Abbey School. Two others had, through my father's endless efforts, gone to O'Connell's school in Dublin and that's where I was heading after first class. I had reached the stage when for the first time I was allowed to do what I was simply dying to do and that was walk down the street of our village with a collection box to get some pennies for the little black babies. The very first fellow I met, I went straight over to him and said, "Can you spare a penny for the little black babies,?" and he said, "I can't, I've six little white ones at home."

### *Sundays*
Our usual family Mass was at 8am and we travelled by horse and trap but the road horse that we had at the time did not appreciate this inconvenience at such an early hour and so was very difficult to catch. A few of us were up the fields by 7am to help get the "mare" as she was called, down to the yard to be harnessed and ready for the trap. We had to bring all the animals, cattle, land horse, donkey, and Shep the faithful sheep

dog also helped. The "mare" was on her guard and protested all the way, kicking and snapping with wide head movements to avoid the winkers. One morning we had to corral her between the front gate and the field gate to try to catch her, but with one run and leap, she cleared the gate and galloped off up the field. It was difficult that morning and we were nearly late for Mass. People arriving from various parts of the parish had a regular spot in the village to tie up their horses, and ours was right at Castletown gate, the home of the Carew family and the estate where for years my father worked as a farm labourer. Sunday afternoons was the time for the drive out the country roads in the trap and this we had to take in turn from one week to the next, as we would never all fit in the rig. I can hear my father saying to those travelling, "You'd better wrap yourself up well if you want to come with us." My mother would always travel and she would have a big rug to fit the length of the trap covering everyone's knees. Going up hills, we were all told to move up to the front as much as possible and going down hill to move towards the back. This assisted the mare in her job. I loved when we'd call to an elderly aunt of ours, because we were always sure of tea and currant cake. Then at a further point we might have to make a stop off at the house of the cobbler who also made harnesses for the horses. There was always something to be delivered or collected. My father loved the country roads and gave us the odd bit of information as we went, while my mother was pre-occupied with keeping us in order. My father would issue an order now and again, "If yuse don't behave yerselves, yis won't come again." I often heard him say, "I know every bump on these roads." I could vouch for that, because he never missed one of them!

**O'Connell School**
As I was only starting second class I was still very young and but for the fact that I already had two older brothers attending the same school, it would have been too complicated for me to travel alone to my new school in Dublin, O'Connell's, in the

north of the city. It was four old pennies to Capel St. and one from there to the school. This was to be my daily journey for the following eleven years. I was another culchie arriving in from Kildare, and I had the record in my class of having the furthest to travel at that time. There were a few other lads also from Celbridge and all of us had a special privilege of being allowed off ten minutes early in order to make the connection at Capel St. otherwise there was a long gap to the next bus. I loved the getting off early bit from the start.

This was my first introduction to the Christian Brothers with their long black dress-like soutanes and leather belt. There were very few lay teachers and these were male. The Brothers were very strict and tough but excellent teachers. I could see even at that stage that it was not merely a job for them but a genuine interest in the pupils and of course, like the nuns, they had a strong religious input. The specially made leather strap, about eighteen inches long, was liberally used right through primary and secondary levels. It became part of life and not a week would pass but I would go home with sore hands and wrists. It was a waste of time complaining at home, and so there was no option but to try and do whatever was asked to avoid as much corporal punishment as possible. Learning was, and continued to be, for me an on-going strenuous effort and when I reached the end of third class, I was told I'd have to repeat that class as the brother did not regard me as fit or good enough for fourth. That was a sickening blow to me as I was made feel down-graded and not able to keep up with my fellow pupils, and worse still, it meant an extra year at school. There was no one available to discuss this with or any encouraging or uplifting words from home or school. All I heard my father say was that I just hadn't the intelligence and the brothers must know what they're doing. My mother always took these events quietly and with very little comment. So, now I was not only the red necked culchie in from the country, but I was the one who "was kept back a year." In a real sense this experience added to my now growing sense of inferiority and this became a real problem for me which I didn't know how to handle. Little did I know that I was to battle with this complex for most of my life to come with only some periods when I felt the relief of self- confidence.

### *Simple happy home life*

There was so much going on at this early stage in my life that I somehow became very attached to home life and all that went with it. We all had our individual chores, like feeding and watering certain animals, checking on the fowl, collecting eggs, opening up or locking up and so on. We were often left with the same job for long periods, as everyone knew then what each had to do and therefore was responsible if anything went wrong. Also emerging was a sense of enterprise that my father established for each of us early in life, in that he would tell us a certain calf, pig, pony or donkey actually belonged to us and depending on how we looked after it and whatever it made when sold, the money would be ours to buy something we needed. That gave a great sense of responsibility, independence and sometimes pride, in the manner we would take care of something which was our own, but especially a terrific feeling of owning something for ourselves. It was a masterpiece of psychology on the part of my father. Looking back, I suppose it was no mere accident that I was allotted the donkey, because not knowing this, in later years, my fellow students abbreviated Eamonn to "Ned" and my class-mates still call me by that name today. But I was proud of this donkey and I immediately called him Nedeen when he was given to me. I managed to get a lovely little cart for him, immaculate harness and was then ready for any big haulage jobs around the farm.

There was nothing I liked more than harvest time when the corn was being brought to the yard and I would try everything to get off school in order to help with my donkey and cart, saying that I could carry as much as any horse and dray. The few times I was allowed to do this, were some of the happiest and most enjoyable days of my life. The night before such a harvest day, knowing I was going to be a full helping hand with my rig next day, I would look out the window for some considerable time before going to bed enjoying the smell of harvest in the air, the clear sky and full moon of the late

August-early-September evening, and I would lie awake for hours thinking of all the corn I was going to bring down from the fields the next day. No helpers were allowed on my rig. I loaded, tied, ferried, and unloaded by myself. My determined nature emerged here, in that I'd keep on going flat out, hardly stopping for a drink or food and I'd be the last that evening to be heard coming down from the fields, my little cart bopping and swaying with the heavy load and it would be twilight or almost fully dark. That actual journey from our top field to the yard with my heavy wheat sheaves rich in grain, was an out of the world, total communication with nature for me, and I thought at the time it was the nearest thing to Heaven I had experienced so far. Also, I felt really important, that I was playing a significant role in doing my bit to save the harvest. There would be no point in telling the "Jackeens" about all of this in school because they would not understand and they'd only laugh at me anyway. But I had a richness and an appreciation inside of me, which I can sense to this very day, fifty years later. It was a period I wished would last forever if possible, but I knew that was only a passing dream. My interests around the farm spread out to other areas, like the beauty of the meadows just before cutting, the wild life out and about, rabbits, hares, birds, foxes, badgers, the flocks of crows and pigeons and I suppose it was the whole world of wild life that could be seen over what was a very small area of land which we owned.

One year the weather at harvest time had been so bad that there was a national emergency and the army was sent out to help save the harvest. There was great excitement and fun when we had a lorry load of soldiers come to us on a Sunday afternoon. Dispensation had been given from the altar to work at the saving even on the Holy Sabbath; and that really indicated the gravity of the situation. No payment was expected, but food was supplied. I never saw as many people in our top field before or since. My mother arrived up pushing a pram (and that was no mean task all the way from the house) full of homemade brown bread, jam, ham, currant cakes and would you believe, a full bucket of tea already sugared and milked. You just dipped your mug into the bucket and you had "instant, ready-to drink" tea. Tea and food like this always tasted much nicer out in the fields, than they would at table in the house. The assembled crowd was a sight to behold and how they enjoyed and very much appreciated the spread my mother had set for them. Some of the lads in the battalion, were city folk and would not have had much experience, if any, of this sort of work, but they enjoyed the food and praised the mother saying, "Be god missus ya must be a great cook to be able to feed an army." And my father would interject and say "It's no bother to her, she's feedin' an army every day o' the week."

I can barely remember the big old steam engine pulling the threshing machine into our yard and that year was to be the last for such engines, as tractors were appearing and taking over. The big engine knocked down the pillars of the gate it was so wide, but that was one of the sacrifices made to get the thrashing done. I simply loved this whole event which usually lasted some days for us. Again my mother was very busy with the tea and homemade bread and my father also supplied the men with some bottles of stout. My job was clearing the chaff away from under the mill. The humming noise of the thrashing mill, the dust, the excitement, the shouting and hollering, could be heard in the whole neighbourhood. The old man in charge of the steam engine, if you saw him today, you would say he was definitely out of the "Ark" with his hob nail boots, trousers tied up with binder twine, an old jacket that was much too small for him, the inevitable cap of course, to top it off, and a white clay pipe with most of the shank broken off. He'd just have the stump in his mouth, and when he had everything up and running, the steam engine full of coal and water (the only fuel ingredients it needed), he then had a most important role to play and that was feeding the corn into the mill from his sitting perch on top. Two lads tossed the sheaves with double grained forks onto the mill, two more cut the twine on them and laid them on the slanted table making sure the head with the grain was facing the correct way, then eased the sheaf in front of the big man in charge (puffing away with the stump of a clay pipe in his mouth) and as he was the expert, he knew the exact rate and volume with which to feed the machine. There was a big commotion one day when one of the lads tossing from the reek was a real bit of a trickster and he nudged his partner and said, "Just watch the big fella feedin' the mill." With that he hurled a sheaf still untied at the big fella, hit him straight in the "kisser" as we called it, knocked the clay pipe out of his mouth and the cap off his head. The sheaf, still untied and in one piece, plus the pipe and cap, all went down into the mill, which made the whole machine jump, groan and then stall. This put the steam engine under a severe surge of pressure and all the workers knew that something had gone wrong. The trickster tried to ignore everything, to give the impression that it was an accident, nothing really to do with him and carried on in a manner oblivious to the whole thing. But the big feeder man at the receiving end of this, was wise and experienced enough, from a whole life time at this work, to know exactly what was going on, and in fact he would have worked with this known trickster before. Well, he stood up, allowing the machine to rumble away idly and at full blast, as he let out a string of curses the likes of which I'd never heard in my life until then. The words were delivered in such a combination and sudden outburst, that I thought the corn would turn red!

Our little holding was originally part of a bigger estate and it was traditional for the annual foxhunt to pass through our place and over the land. A passage would normally be made for them. I think it was either part of the deal with the Land Commission and the so-called gentry, or it was just part of the old descendency stemming from the penal days. There was still the attitude of landlord and tenant. Anyway, local farmers, including ourselves made way for them by opening gates, making suitable jumping fences over the land and allowed a way through for them, their horses and hounds. One man riding with the pack, who was himself a local farmer, would flick my father a half dollar, and of course he was regarded as the only decent man among them. I fancied the challenge myself to try and be part of all this, and so had my Nedeen all groomed and ready, riding bare back, waiting at the haggard gate and then took off after the hunt up through our first field. When I reached the first fence which by now had been negotiated long ago by all the others, "my mount" refused even to attempt the jump and my short-lived hunting days abruptly came to an end.

On an occasional year, when the turf might be in short supply, it would be decided to fell a tree for firewood and all hands were required to help get the logs down to the shed. Of course "my rig" was put to valuable use once again. On one such occasion, the tree being felled was on a bank neighbouring a farmer who in fact was Russian, married to an upper class English lady, and when the sound of the cross-cut rang out, the lady of the house next door came over to the boundary. She claimed that the tree we were cutting was in fact on their side of the ditch, which was not true at all, and she claimed further that she had lived for so many long years to see those beautiful trees right along the fence grow to what they were today. My father's answer was, "Well Maam, if you stay there for just another half hour, you'll see this one kiss the ground." The work continued and she went off saying she was on her way to call the Garda. The tree was already on the ground, when right enough we spotted the local sergeant walking across the field heading our way pushing his bike. The old lady was out again standing in the middle of her field to witness the arrival of the law. She was well out of range to hear what the sergeant said to my father, which was, "God bless the work men and all here. Listen, I had to put in an appearance when I got the call, but don't you mind that auld bitch out there one bit, just drop me down a few logs sometime, and ye won't hear another word about this."

The year when a bank of turf was acquired, a number of us would be transported to the site by taking a hitch in a lorry and between the cutting, footing, drying and then stacking near the road, the whole operation would take about two weeks, during which time we would have a nearby hay barn as our sleeping quarters at night and live mostly on rabbit stew. These were shot by my older brother who was allowed to have and use a single barrel shotgun. These were good, healthy, fun days and were a complete change of scene with a whole lot of freedom.

Talking of rabbits, I started a little business of my own, when I got into pet rabbits, mostly white or black and white. I began to breed and rear them, and then sell them to a pet shop in Capel St. for a half dollar each. The man in the shop would sell them on for five shillings. I had boxes, netting wire fences and runs all through the apple trees as that was one area which didn't need tilling. By moving the runs regularly, I had sufficient grass for them and they in turn helped to control the grass through the trees. The old man in charge of the steam engine I spoke of earlier, used to visit our place quite often and was a wise old adviser to everybody. He would check on all that was happening around the little farmyard. He always asked me about the rabbits, how many I had, (as many as thirty one time) and what price I was getting and so on. One day when he questioned me, I told him some rabbits had broken out of their run (no one to blame but me of course) and I'd got all of them back except one, our cat had caught and killed it. "Bring me that cat and I'll teach her a lesson," he said. Thinking he was going to give her a few slaps and thumps, I unwittingly brought him my mother's prize cat which was not only a great ratter but she loved and cherished it also. He took the cat by the ears, flicked his blackthorn stick at the back of her ears, and then said to me, "Bury her, she won't kill any more of your rabbits." She was as dead as a door nail. I got such a fright, I'll never forget it. I could not believe this cat, now in my hands, was dead merely by a quick expert flick of the stick behind the ear. What was my mother going to say? I would have sacrificed all the bloody rabbits, just to have the cat alive again.

I wasn't as fortunate as an older brother who ventured into breeding and selling pigeons to the same pet shop, but selling them, not once or twice but several times, the same pigeons over and over again. It was a similar little project to mine but had this one remarkable advantage of being able to recycle the same stock several times, (unfortunately for me, rabbits couldn't fly!). When the birds were fully feathered and fledged he would deliver them to the Capel St. shop, collect his money, and within not more than a week, the pigeons would be back to their place of birth. Being of the homing nature, it was no bother to them to find their way home from wherever they were sold out to, in the greater city area. The pet shop man did not know they were the same birds, when a new batch were presented for sale. My brother had a bit of a conscience about this, but then again he thought it was a perk of the business he was in. So he decided one season to test the homing ability of the birds by not allowing them out of the box until he brought them to the pet shop. To everyone's amazement, while it took a little longer, nearly a month, they were back. My father got to hear what was going on and said this was not on and had to stop immediately. He was like that, very straight.

### *The fun days*
With eight boys and two girls, fun, games and the surprise tricks were never far away. I always wished to be part of this, but sometimes found it difficult to get on the inner circle of what might be brewing. I had a distinct impression of being somewhat singled out because of the future now beginning to take shape for me and while my parents would fairly often refer to the subject of me going to be the future priest in the family, a sort of atmosphere was created, at least I thought so, which made me feel apart, different, not expected to be part of

the ordinary run of the mill, and therefore allowances should be made when and where necessary. I did not like this one little bit because I wanted to be part of everything that was going on; to feel I was one of the lads and that I was capable of being part of the risks and sometimes daring things that often occurred.

Halloween was a great occasion for family fun which was simple, enjoyable, and harmless in many ways. I clearly remember the variety of nuts, some of which we'd pick from trees on our own fields and other games such as: the apple dangling from the twine and with hands tied behind your back you had to take a bite out of it to claim it; trying to get the three penny piece out of the basin of water by mouth only; blind man buff games; dressing up in all sorts of old clothes and calling to neighbours. It was not just one day or night, we used to drag it out for days and sometimes weeks, especially when playing tricks on some passers-by. The parcel and the string up the tree was one I learned myself from an old man, and I got great mileage out of it. The idea was that I'd make up an attractive parcel about the size of a shoe box, all nicely wrapped, tie a strong piece of string around it, then using the bow of an over-hanging tree to the road as a type of pulley, I could pull the parcel quickly up the tree and out of sight. I'd be all set with the parcel on the road, the string suspended and I'd hide just waiting for the next cyclist to come and there were plenty of them. Invariably ninety percent would first pass the parcel by a good few yards, and having noticed it, would pull into the side, get off the bike, and slowly turn around hoping no one was watching, but found that the parcel had just disappeared. There would be the scratching of the head, pushing the cap back, looking around into the ditch, having a face of bewilderment, and then maybe feeling a little foolish, before eventually retrieving the bike and slowly heading off. It was extremely difficult not to burst out laughing, especially if there were a few of us behind the tree. I used a similar fun trick one April fool's day, but did not use the string. The parcel was on the road and when someone stopped to pick it up, all would shout "April fool!" and watch the variety of reactions from the victim. I had made a parcel with a rotten turnip inside and succeeded in stopping our single-decker C.I.E. bus full of people, and heard the driver shout at the conductor, "There's a parcel on the road." He got out and walked back, with all the people watching and wondering what was going on. I waited for him to pick it up and as he began to shake it and examine it with all eyes on him, from my hiding place deep in the ditch, I shouted out " April fool!" which got a great laugh from his driver and all on the bus. He was furious and just like a cricket bowler he hurled the parcel in the direction of my voice, then jumped back on the bus in great embarrassment. Nobody but I knew what a good shot it was. This large soft missile hit me with full impact and the contents of the rotten turnip sprayed me better than a muck spreader could do. My trick back-fired and not a single person but me ever knew about that. I had some cleaning up job to do.

Another one I learned and I was likely to use it any time of the year, was putting a tiny piece of carbide into a small tin, something like a mustard box, then punch a hole in the bottom, release in some spittle, fix the lid on tightly, and when ready to shock the passing motorist or cyclist, put a lighted match to the hole in the bottom, then a loud bang would follow as the lid was blown off. Having become somewhat of an expert at this trick, it too backfired on me one day. I was forever losing the lids after the bang, so I invented a way of saving them, by tying it with a piece of string to the main tin box, and at first it worked very successfully, but the fateful day arrived when I was launching my "surprise attack" on a motor cyclist and the flying lid with string attached got caught in his wheel and then pulled the entire tin box from my hand. I just ran to the yard, hid behind the hay stack and to my horror the noise of a motor bike came rumbling all over the place with a very angry rider. I could hear him speak to one of my brothers, saying he was looking for the little "git" who nearly knocked him off his bike with this stupid tin box which he held in his hand. I was sinking deeper into the hay, as my brother insisted he knew nothing about it, but he knew quite well it was me. Soon the bike roared off, as the rider shouted "I'll get the Garda." I praised the brother as I emerged. He was unhappy to be landed in this spot but we vowed on our usual phrase when a secret needed to be kept among family members, saying, "mum's the word."

I was always into trying some new experiment with an angle of fun in it and as I was learning my first steps in physics at school, the power of confined steam amazed me. So one afternoon as I was doing a regular chore of burning all the waste boxes and paper from the shop, I decided to experiment. I put a small amount of water in a strong five gallon oil drum with the lid firmly sealed and placed this on the big fire. I waited patiently for over an hour but no explosion had occurred and with the fire now slowly burning itself out, I was disappointed that the drum had not blown up. Just then, it rolled over and I heard a groan of expanding metal. On the nearby road I noticed two nuns were out for their afternoon walk unaware of my experiment nearby. As I sheltered behind an apple tree, there followed a very loud explosion which in turn sent a cloud of smoke and ashes high into the sky. I never saw nuns run like the two out on the road. On being asked inside the house later what the bang was, I claimed to know nothing about it.

Some years had now passed and I emerged with bitter disappointment and sadness from the realization of who the real Santa Claus was, and this period stands out as a very painful time, because I did not wish to let it go. However it was similar to an illness, it healed. We still got our small Christmas presents which were mostly wooden toys roughly hammered together at first by my father, but in later years, my eldest brother who was an aspiring carpenter and produced some new and interesting exhibits. Very often if there was a lot of pressure to get things finished on time, older items would just disappear near the dead line, and reappear, modified and a different colour.

Although we didn't always exchange presents among family members, everyone did with the parents and of course they with us. The coppers were scarce for us and so the presents simple and meagre. I can clearly remember my first effort of a present to my father and mother, he got a box of matches and she got one handkerchief. The gratitude and appreciation from them both was memorable and on receiving their gift they would say it was the very thing they needed, clearly conveying to the presenter, that special thought and effort must have been expended on arranging this gift. All this exchange of pleasantries with the many other Christmas effects about the house, created a deeply true and lasting spirit of the Christmas season.

### *Childhood days*
A lot of responsibilities piled on because of the status of being in sixth class, and with the prospect of sitting the big Primary Certificate examination. If successful one became eligible to go into the secondary level. Of course, making one's Confirmation was merely part of that whole stage in schooling and up-bringing. Being in the sixth class group we were regarded as the elite of the primary level and were all finely tuned by the sharpest and best teachers available. They pushed each pupil to the limit of their capabilities, and if they couldn't produce the goods, then no one could. They did not hesitate in using corporal, intimidating, humiliating and sometimes downright abusive verbal methods. I often thought the verbal onslaughts were more hurtful and effective than were the physical. It seemed there was an all out push to extract the best possible results from the potential talent on hand. So, school in sixth class was a high-powered, gruelling type of year. The thinking behind these methods by the teachers and principals, was that quite a few pupils would be leaving general education at the end of this year and going on to learn

a trade in the then developing Technical Schools. Each school tried to produce the best possible results and so maintain a high standard in the public arena. I struggled in my usual way to keep up with this class work and homework which became a priority for all pupils. One particular brother had a fast moving method of examining History in class. He would start at the top with some period we should know all about and going very quickly through the class each boy would have to give, in just a few words, the next detail in the sequence of events. When it came to me, this certain king we were discussing had been executed, and my contribution should have been that George, James or Willie, whatever his name was, had been beheaded. When asked what happened next, what did I say? "He was headed." This got a huge guffaw from the class to my great embarrassment.

The Confirmation took place fairly early in the year, so as not to distract too much from the big exam. While First Holy Communion was and always will be a life time memory, Confirmation on the other hand for me can only be described as "a non event." Yes, we got our new suits and for the first time we were allowed to wear long trousers, which of course gave a great sense of being grown up and of being a man. Looking occasionally at the class photo of that period, I can see all the young men, as they were then, with their own particular characteristics and idiosyncrasies which very interestingly don't really change in the individual over many years. I say this, because in meeting some of them years later at a wedding or function of some sort and conversing with them, the same personality still comes across as was there in primary school. We were confirmed, not in our own home parish church, but in the local parish church in which our school was situated. We arrived to school that morning all dressed in our new suits and long trousers, sporting the big red Confirmation badge, and then marched off to the church to take our places with many pupils from other surrounding schools. No member of any family was present, just some brothers, teachers and priests of the parish. The doors were closed to the general public and we awaited the arrival of the bishop. Every second row of seats was left vacant to leave room for the bishop to pass through while picking boys at random to ask them some catechism question.

This was frightening and didn't lend itself in anyway to the solemnity or significance of the occasion. While the ceremony was mostly in Latin, small parts were in English. A teacher was the sponsor for his entire class and the bishop gave the so called "dreaded" slap on the cheek. This was a mere passing tap which was symbolic in becoming soldiers for Christ, but of course a " big deal", was made out of this by some in the class, as if the bishop was going to bash us all. The confirming bishop was the relatively new Archbishop J.C. McQuaid, and one of the priests had the boys on alert warning that he just might ask someone his name, to see if they knew the new leader in the Church. To help boys remember, the priest told them to think of the tobacco a lot of people smoked, "Mick McQuade." True to expectation the Archbishop did ask in his quiet, almost inaudible voice, "Would you know my name?" The young fella shouted out "Mick McQuade". Well the priest clenched his fists as if ready to box the young lad and you could almost read his grinding teeth and quivering lips, saying "Ya dirty little eejit, ya got it all wrong." We returned to school after the ceremony for class photos and had a relaxed hour or so and then were allowed to go home and spend the rest of the day with our family.

That was it and that's what I mean when I say Confirmation was a non-event, as far as I was concerned. I rose in rank in another field when I became head altar boy, and of course the news of "me going to be the priest", had now spread far and wide and as they say was talked about in the market place. There was no question of me quitting the altar as other boys did after sixth class, because I was going to need all this as part of my on-going training. Being in charge or being a leader never did, even to this day mean anything to me as far as superiority is concerned. I must say being part of the large family and the teamwork that went with it stood to me in that regard.

There was a priest in our home church at one period who had been a late vocation and had come from the school teaching world. One morning while serving Mass I had moved a book from one spot to another at the wrong time and when we came in to the sacristy, he gave me such a slap across the cheek I became dizzy. I was bitterly disappointed with this and the image of the priest fell in my estimation to a pitiful low. If, while on the altar I had been misbehaving myself, talking, laughing or as they say "messin," well then there would have been some slightly more acceptable angle to this punishment, but for making a simple rubrical error, I really felt it was uncalled for. Coming from a priest who had just celebrated Mass, and the pedestal on which I placed him, I just could not for the life of me understand it. There was no point in saying anything at home, because the answer would be the usual, that I must have deserved it and the priest had to be right. I never told anyone.

About this time I began to show interest in learning to play the violin or as we called it, the fiddle. My father had one and sometimes played an odd tune for us or for visitors. You must have an ear for music to play the fiddle because it's an instrument where you have to make the notes with the fingers and not just press a key. My father sang a little and his favourite was "The Rose of Moon Coyne." A smaller fiddle was acquired for me and I began to take lessons. This was to be the beginning of dabbling with many instruments but not sticking long enough with any particular one to become any good at it.

### *Home scenes*
On the home front more responsibilities were allotted to me and like many things that come our way in life, some you welcome and some you don't. I found myself in charge of the

weekly Saturday evening bath time for the younger ones. This eight foot long and two foot wide bath made of tin with two big handles at either end would be placed in front of the fire in our general purpose room, and while taking my own bath I would include two or three of the smaller ones with me while my mother was heating gallons of water in big metal pots on the range. My job was to make sure the water was an even temperature, not too cold and not too hot, and to shout out when needed. As towels were not plentiful, we all did a drip-dry job beside the fire, then we got into our nightclothes, prepared for the final check over by my mother of face, hair, nails and backs of the ears especially.

As there was no running water in the house, there was no bathroom and the toilet was a small section of an out shed which as you can imagine was a very busy department first thing every morning. The toilet paper was strips of old newspapers and the emptying of the large bucket was a chore that moved from one to another every day. Our supply of water was from a well, situated between the second and top fields and was pumped by hand into milk churns and ferried down by horse and cart. This well also watered all the animals and again we took turns at the tedious and laborious pumping job to insure that the troughs were constantly topped up. These were in fact old heavy discarded baths from a gentry house and were propped up by stones on either side. While helping one day, my younger brother stood with his hand over the side of one of the troughs, while I kept the pump handle going. With no warning the second trough moved from its unsteady base support and jammed right against his fingers. This action cut off the top of his middle finger. He ran towards the yard screaming and bleeding profusely. Before following him, I managed to move the trough, and the finger top, complete with nail, dropped to the ground. I picked it up and ran after him. He was already in the house being tended to by my mother, and the district nurse was on her way. I brought the severed finger-top straight to my father, thinking sensibly enough that it might possibly be stitched back on. My father was stoking a big fire in the middle of the yard with pots of food cooking for some animals and when I gave him the piece of finger, he just threw it in the fire without even considering what I thought was a brilliant idea, and said, "Get off outa that, what good is that yoke now." Anyway the finger did grow back, complete with a new nail.

My mother entrusted me with the job of going to the grocery shop in the village for the weekly supply of items which could not be home-supplied, things like sugar, tea etc. and for fear I'd forget anything I had to keep on repeating the list over and over in my mind. Part of this job was calling to a local lady-farmer who supplied us with some extra eggs in return for brown bread. Having collected the eggs I then saw a possible short cut home across the fields, instead of the wide circuit by road. While trying to negotiate a barbed wire fence with my cargo of messages, I slipped and got caught in the thorny wire. I was left suspended, head down and dangling from the five foot-high fence, caught by the back of my leg. I resembled a circus trapeze act, only my support was the barbed wire cutting deep into the back of my knee. There was no one within sight or sound and in considerable pain and distress, I wondered if I was going to be left there for the night and possibly bleed to death. Eventually I managed to scramble back up and was able to release my leg and slip to the ground, where I lay for quite a while trying to regroup myself and muster strength to finish the journey home. By the time I got there I was limping badly and my knee was severely swollen. There was no way I could hide my predicament and had to reveal exactly what happened. While I got immediate first aid attention from my mother, who washed and bandaged my knee, the district nurse was called to do a professional job and to give me an anti-tetanus injection. The sympathy extended at home was "That'll teach ya not to take short cuts in the future."

My mother seemed to be forever in the house, except when going to Mass or some devotions, or out on the Sunday afternoon drive. There was little enough time lag between us ten, so her poor body was under constant pressure either with house work, or in the process of pregnancy. Despite all this demanding work she was always there in a special way for a sick child. I often thought she was some kind of wonder woman or a magician, because she could produce a dinner from an empty pot. It seemed to me that at any time of the day there was always food cooking or ready for serving. There was not much hugging and kissing at home even on occasions when you might have need of it. Everyone was too busy doing things; and if you weren't doing things, you were not pulling your weight around the place. It's not that there wasn't any love, there was, but it was not always available or expressed. I suppose as a result we all grew in a manner, lacking the means and the wherewithal of expressing love to others. This was something each one of us had to learn for ourselves down the road in life.

Just as we had our jobs out and about the farmyard, we also had our work to do in the house, such as sweeping, dusting and washing and putting away of the delft after the main meals. It was some picture when all twelve were around the table. My mother could not stock up quick enough, for as soon as she'd leave a plate of anything down, it was not worth her while taking her hand off, it would be cleared immediately, and off she'd go for another fill. This was especially true if we were coming in after some work out in the fields, like picking spuds, thinning turnips, weeding carrots. While we ravenously devoured the food my mother always kept a very strict watch over table manners and how to use the cutlery properly, and ask for something to be passed, rather than stretch over another. The last rule I broke one day by stretching and not asking for something to be passed. My mother said, "Have you no tongue in your head?" I thought I'd be really smart and funny by saying, "It wouldn't reach that far Ma." Well, she drew out and gave me such a belt across the back of the neck, I nearly choked on the food in my mouth. "That'll teach ya to get smart with me, ya bucko," she said.

One day my older sister and I were detailed to do the wash up after dinner as it was our turn. A problem arose when neither of us wished to do the drying because that meant the person drying had to put away also, and would be last to get out to play. Both of us being stubborn, neither would give in or compromise and a chase around the huge table packed with dirty dishes ensued. My sister followed me with a long knotted dishcloth and attempted to hit me each time we circled. We went round and round getting faster and faster, until she made one last swipe at me whereupon I fell on the corner of the range, splitting my eye open. She had hit the corner of the table severely and the leg broke bringing most of the dishes crashing down, breaking on the floor. As I lay crying and bleeding from the eye, she ran and climbed up the branches of a nearby tree and then to really make a nightmare out of the whole affair, she fell off and broke her arm. We both ended up being patched and nursed rather than punished.

One Saturday, we were stacking the hay in the haggard, and I was privileged to be up on top of the reek helping to build and shape it, when there was a loud call that the dinner was ready. There was a scramble for the house like a stampede of wild animals. All of us were very high up and some used a ladder to descend, but I decided to slide down the side of the hay reek, not knowing someone had left a fork right at the spot where I was to reach the ground. Fortunately, it was the handle that was up and not the spiked grains. This handle hit me, as if it were an upper cut from a heavy weight boxer and I just went out cold. I woke up lying on the sofa and the very first words I heard came from my father which were, "He won't be able to go to the pictures tonight." That was the best cure that could have been issued. I was up and about instantly, saying, "I'm all right, I'm all right."

Yes the little cinema in Lucan was the big night out for all of us. We had a little baby Ford van by now and we packed into the back like sardines. No one wished to miss what we called "the follyer upper" every Saturday night. Coming out from the cinema we'd have been left in a state of severe suspense. The cut would come at a very crucial stage for the "good guy" or "the chap" and the talk all the way home and during the week, would be about how he was going to get out of his predicament. But before going home, we had a further treat, a visit to the chipper across the road where a man called "Feleechi" had lovely chips. Normally we would just get a bag each and eat them on the way home. But this particular night, we thought we'd go up market, and go for the plate and fork service for our chips, and if you did this, the rule was you had to sit at the table and eat inside. But when we had our helping on plates, there were no tables available, so we decided to sit around the van outside and eat away. One of our gang dropped and broke a plate and we thought there was no point in going back in with an extra fork and a plate less. It was decided at the "around the van conference" to leave a fork short as well, so as not to arouse suspicion. But we were about to pull away, when our Italian chipper man, "Feleechi," came running out, saying, "There's one fork and one plate missing; the fork will cost three shillings, and the plate will probably cost you all six months in jail." It got sorted out somehow and as we set out on the three mile journey home we encountered our next door neighbour returning from the greyhound track with his racing dogs in the big old brown V8 van. We dared our brother driver to tease him into a race. That was something, with all of us "whooshing" on the van in our neck and neck encounter all the way to the gate at the incredible speed of forty miles per hour.

Our house at this stage had been connected with electricity and our first radio arrived in a big box. A tractor with spade lugs was beginning to replace the horses; bits and pieces of machinery appeared and the whole place was taking on the shape of a new phase. More independence grew with the advent of mowing machines and binders for corn cutting. I loved when I had the job of sitting on the machine controlling and checking that everything was operating, but very often I abandoned my post to chase rabbits escaping from the crop. When grazing grass was in short supply, we took our turn minding the cattle while they grazed on the roadside. This was called the long acre. Often territory had to be defended from intruding neighbours, and I witnessed my father detailing an older brother to go and fist fight a fellow on the middle of the road, because he had allowed his two donkeys to enter our patch of the long acre. After sparring for a while, my father told the two of them to go home, they were hopeless; he'd seen better scraps between game cocks.

Everyone was beginning to get on with their own lives with whatever they decided to do. My father had branched out into dealing in secondhand furniture and by now owned a small store in the village. My mother opened a small grocery shop. Among my brothers and sisters various careers were emerging, a carpenter, mechanic, tailor, farmer, a nun and a priest, all by now in the making. It was while going to the auctions with my father, that I learned a bit about antiques. Our back shed had to be extended to store and repair the growing furniture stock required. It was here I learned to finger a few tunes on a pedal harmonium in my spare time. But the value of the pound was still evident, when after helping a man to repair a puncture one day, my father had a one pound note stuffed into his top pocket, and he ran to my mother delighted as he said, "Look what the man is after giving me." This one note would have bought most of our groceries for a week.

## CHAPTER TWO

## HOME AND SCHOOL - PART II

**My Father and Mother**
I remember as a very young boy in my innocence asking a mother of thirteen children which of them she loved the best, and she gave me a very wise answer; "The one who's sick." When I look back on all ten of us and our relationship with our parents, there were no favourites, even the two girls were treated equally. However if there was one sick or in need of any sort, then special attention was given to that one, but only while the need lasted. Thank God, there was no on-going illness for anyone in our house at that time, just the ordinary run of the mill happenings.
The relationship between the children and parents was typical of the era we lived in and nothing extraordinary stood out. My father and mother said many times, "There must be no house in the whole of Ireland like this one," to highlight or emphasize some event because it was so bad or because it was so good. They were both brilliant providers, especially as we had so little. They had a total sense of unselfish dedication and literally everything they had went to the family. When it came to try and pay for our education this put enormous strain on the whole budget. I so often heard them say, "We'll make it some how," and they did. There was the usual go-between approach, when someone wanted something, or sought permission to go somewhere. My mother was often approached first, with the thinking that if she asked him, my father would not refuse. He

always had the final decision and no one dared to try and change that. Serious disobedience was rare while all were under age and anyway the scope was very limited as to what to do and where to go. Football, skittles or ice skating on the road in winter, were some of the pastimes. My father had a great sense of pride and expectation in everyone doing very well in future life and he encouraged us all in whatever way he could. My mother on the other hand would regularly use her well known phrase, "When the apple is ripe, it falls." In many ways she had a more passive attitude and was less complimentary of any success but in her own quiet way she delighted in the achievements of the family.

Between father and mother themselves, there was a solid, practical and understanding kind of love. We would never hear terms of endearment such as, "sweetie," "darling" or "beloved" exchanged between them, but we sensed a happy, healthy relationship that worked. We knew by the tone of voice they used and the way they called each other by their pet names that there was a great closeness between them. They cut the image of the swans perfectly, together for life. They prayed, laughed, worked and worried together and although we never saw it, I'm sure they cried together. While we all got our knuckles wrapped and ears pulled at times, there was never any violence as such in our house. My father never once raised his hand to my mother, although they had their arguments. They were tough, I'll have to say that and brought us up with a battling spirit no matter what came along. We never knew our grandparents, on either side, as they were dead before my father and mother ever met.

While neither referred very much to our grandparents, they did mention occasionally that there was a history of alcohol problems on both sides, and so there was a fear of it in the air and our house was practically alcohol free. My father often said to us to be careful of the drink because it was in the blood. A later chapter on this subject will prove him right when I come to discuss my own experience and struggle. While he took a drink himself and often came home from the cattle market with a good few bottles of stout on board, he was never arrogant or violent towards anyone. In fact he only wished to have fun, sing and tell stories. Sometimes when he'd have an old friend back with him, we'd all sit around the fire listening with great interest to the long drawn out and often exaggerated descriptions of their earlier days fighting for the country and what should and shouldn't be done. There was one man in particular we loved to see, because he was in the military jail with my father and had lost an arm at some meeting of his organization. A hand grenade was thrown in the window and as he went to throw it out, it blew up. Every time he came, we made him tell that story. We knew it off by heart, and also insisted on examining his steel hook which he had protruding from his sleeve. Then we would turn to our father who would be in flying form by now, to tell of his escape from jail and he'd be told not to forget the "fella and his shoe." He'd look over at my mother and she from her knitting basket would give a look of disapproval with an expression on her face which seemed to say, "Oh no, not that again." The chorus would get louder and more insistent. Conscious of the presence of his pal and jail mate, he'd launch off with his usual "beat about the bush" introduction telling us how they had planned the break for weeks and how they'd do it and who was going with them etc. But the part we waited patiently for was the actual night time escape. "There were about ten of us," he'd continue, "we all managed to get out the window and sneak across the yard to the wire. It was cut rapidly with the great yoke we had, and then we had to sneak a long way in the grass to get clear of the search lights. We were doing well until the "eejit" behind me struck a match. "What are ya doin' that for?" he was asked and the answer, was "I'm lookin' for me shoe." "F...k yer shoe, put out that match, we'll all be caught." What a burst of laughter there was. Then in comes my mother of course, "That's grand language in front of the childer." A song or two followed with about twenty odd verses in each. There was encouragement of "good man" every now and then to keep the singer going.

My mother tolerated my father's drinking for the most part until one day he over did it. There was no sign of him for his dinner, he was the only one missing. Leaving the rest of us there eating ours, my mother left her own dinner on the table, never said a word, just put on her old working overcoat and went walking to the village. She went straight into the pub where he was having a great time. She literally got him by the ear lobe and pulled him out and still had him by the ear when she landed him in the chair in front of us all. We hadn't moved. I must say, we were quite frightened more by my mother with her red-faced determination. She said, "Look what you're doin' to the lot of us," she was nearly crying but held back. He then made a loud statement, which I remember to this very day, "Kate I'll never drink again." He never did and kept his pledge for the remaining thirty years of his life. He was quite happy for the years that followed to sit by the fire in the evening, have his smoke, read the newspaper and listen to the radio news. His hobby came in very useful, i.e. having all sorts of caged birds, such as canaries, finches and linnets. He eventually built an aviary and had some prize-winners. While it might seem that the woman took a back seat role in life in those days, in our case my mother came to the rescue in a big way and saved, not only their own relationship, but the welfare of the entire family.

### *The teenager*

I reached the peak of my long climb up the mountain by passing the Primary Certificate Examination. I felt like a thrashed donkey after a long haul, but was rewarded with the sense of achievement and the view I now had of the horizon spread out in front of me, but this too was decked with peaks, to be conquered, a misty fog to be contended with, and a sense of not being adequately equipped for the virtually unknown out there. Nevertheless there was only one way to go and that was forward.

I was still struggling deeply on a personal level, not only in my best efforts to learn and memorize, but also trying to come to terms with what religion, God and all that surrounded these, meant to me as an individual and mind you I was fighting a lone and very difficult battle here. To add to all of this as well as being constantly reminded of my "culchie" status, personal hygiene presented a problem because with such huge demands on my much over-worked mother, it was difficult to provide clean clothes on a regular basis. Underwear was not available at all and so possibly wearing the same trousers and no underpants, for months on end, naturally led to an aroma so other boys would not wish to sit beside me. Added to that, I may have come straight from a farmyard chore and carried with me some manure on my big hob nail boots and so that further added to the air in the classroom. But it was the former problem with my clothes that really made things most difficult and embarrassing for me. There was simply nothing I could do about it. I could not and did not seek preferential treatment and so battled on, knowing that things could only improve in time. I felt very much alone at this time, little knowing that this would be the case for most of my life.

Becoming a teenager and launching into secondary school level, were not all that traumatic, in that I was in the same school, had mostly the same class mates, and the same eleven mile journey by bus each day. I now sensed a more acceptable attitude from teachers and brothers, in that they seemed to treat us as grown-ups, and not just children anymore. The leather strap was still around and was used quite liberally. By now however, we were expected to take punishment like a man.

Personal hygiene had improved immensely and there was a sense of pride in personal appearance; the hair, suit, shirts, socks, shoes (not boots anymore) were all part of a new appearance. This obviously created a certain psychological uplifting for me as an individual, but I was still a very shy, withdrawn, and almost introverted young lad and was lacking in any real confidence even in the company of my own peers. I had this image of myself as not being at all attractive to any other person, male or female; a lad with a big head of red hair in from the country, "ploughing" as it were through the Dublin scene. Neither from school, home or anywhere else, did we receive any mention of sex instruction. If the phrase "age of puberty" was to be put before me, I would not have the slightest idea what it meant. As a teenager I did not understand the huge physiological changes that were going on within my body. It was only at that stage I was asking where I came from. This question is asked at a much earlier age today, and furthermore, answers are given. The answer received from parents was the stock one given to all boys and girls of this age at the time, viz. from under the head of cabbage. I often visited our vegetable garden and there was not one cabbage I hadn't examined carefully for any signs that might indicate the truth in what I was hearing. I continued to press for more facts and details at home, but it was still the same answer with no further comment and I was told not to ask anymore. School did not help either. I was afraid that maybe I'm supposed to know already and that I'd make a fool of myself once again for being so ignorant. People often asked if I had heard about the birds and the bees yet? I hadn't a clue what they meant. I began to watch with interest, not just birds and bees, but all animals and plant life; thinking that I might get some clue. Out of the blue one day, a boy my own age and of a different religion, without me asking him, told me that babies came as a result of a man and woman having some sort of close physical interaction, and a baby then grew inside the woman's tummy for many months before being born. Without spelling out the intimate details of the act, I had for the first time heard the true facts of the matter from a most unexpected source. But I was reasonably satisfied and eased off on my questioning, but sexual curiosity, as I was to learn, is a life long, on-going and deep human instinct. At least my mother's visits to the hospital when there was a new baby coming into the family, or when the cow was having a calf, or the horse a foal, and my rabbits (who are masters at the reproductive process), were all beginning to make sense to me now. But I had to deal with my own personal development and instinctive urges and in some way to put them into the context of where I was at and where I was going. Not only was there a lack of formal sex instruction at any level, but the very mention of the word was almost taboo. The constant pulpit thumping on the sixth and ninth Commandments, the long queues at the confessional by people concerned about their "bad thoughts" and the inability of parents (who themselves had no sex education) to deal with such questions, all led to the belief that "sex" was a dirty word and any discussion on it was bad and dirty talk. So I grew up from here with a rather misleading and certainly very confusing concept in my mind on the whole area of sexuality. Like so many people my so-called sex education was associated with jokes and lurid stories constantly being told among fellow pupils.

At this stage I was experiencing a natural instinctive attraction to the opposite sex and began to wonder whether there would be a response if I made a move. My scope and opportunity were very limited, but one day on the long journey by bus coming from school, I sat beside a local girl whom I knew, and fancied somewhat and wondered if she saw anything in me. I thought I'd try my hand at chatting her up. I was happy that a reasonable mutual conversation was maintained throughout the journey, only to be shattered, when I turned to get off and saw that my father had been standing at the back of the bus and observed closely that I'd been talking to this girl all the way home. The bus was only pulling away when he launched into me saying, "If you want to be a priest, you can't be going on like that, chatting up girls everyday; now make up your mind one way or the other." This continued at home for some time in front of my mother but I never uttered one word. Confused thoughts ran through my head. Did I say I wished to be a priest?......not once do I remember......is this the opening I've

been waiting for?...... he was in a way giving me a choice....
but he wasn't really.....it was just his way of throwing the ball
into my court.....this could be the time....to stand up and let it
be my choice......or maybe otherwise.....there was a lump in
my tummy...I couldn't eat dinner. The point is I enjoyed
talking to that girl and she responded favourably. I didn't care,
I wanted to talk to her again, but I'd check the back of the bus
first. I knew I had a lot of love inside me and not only did I
wish to share it, but I was also looking for some sort of a return
of that love. It was the only means I knew of at this time of a
mutual exchange of love but a relationship with this girl (and
that was not to be) or with any girl for that matter was not to be
the way forward for me. I had this deep urge to explore this
area of growth and development and to leave the air clear for a
decision I so much wished to make myself. Although the signs
I sought were to appear in time at certain stages along the way,
this love-seeking battle was to go on for many years.

### *War, school, religion, politics*
All through the years up to the age of nine and ten, I was little
aware of the Second World War and its atrocities which had
been raging all over Europe especially the persecution of the
Jewish people. Ireland was a neutral country and therefore
was not directly involved but obviously felt the effects of the
war in many ways and the things I remember most were the use
of coupons for the rationing of food stuffs and the sparse
availability of many products needed in the economy. But still
we got by, due in many ways to the fact that we were almost
self-sufficient on our little farm. Except for a few items like
tea, sugar, flour, margarine and the likes, we had everything
else homemade and my father was always very proud when we
all sat around the large rectangular table like the twelve
apostles, if all were present. Any one who complained about
not liking a certain vegetable on the plate, had his or her dinner
taken away immediately and told to get off outside and my
father would be heard saying, "Hunger is good sauce, you'll

like it tomorrow." He had worked too hard with his own sweat and grit providing food for the table. So I and all of us learned very rapidly to do as the Dublin man would say, "Shut your mouth and eat your dinner."

A lot of men smoked the pipe then and of course wore a cap and old photos show most men wearing head gear of some sort. Knowing my father to have certain contacts in the public arena one old man who used the white clay pipe wondered if he (my father) could get him some tobacco which was almost impossible to find anywhere. It so happened at that time, that Bord Na Mona had just produced a new product from the turf on our bogs, called the "briquette" which was a compressed block of turf to give a more lasting fire. One of the many fun instincts of my father then emerged when he gave this old man one of the briquettes and told him it was a new and special tobacco that these German fellas had invented and it was meant to be great stuff. Off the old man went delighted, saying that he'd never seen a piece of tobacco that big. On his next visit, I remember it well, the first question the man was asked was, "How did ya get on with that tobacco?" "Great," he said, "It was very strong and very hard to cut." Believe it not, he had actually smoked the whole of it.

Day and night huge fleets of fighting and bomber planes rumbled across the sky and at night it was like a spectacular laser-like show with all the search lights keeping a constant watch on the elements, which we could clearly see from the nearby army base at Baldonnel. A mile in the Dublin direction from our house, there was a small private air strip developing for flying instruction purposes called Weston, and at night a few of us used to go down there with our then "state of the art" dynamo powered lights on our bikes. One fellow would frantically hand-pedal with the rear wheel lifted off the ground, the other would shine what we thought was a very powerful light into the sky, hoping we might attract or tantalizingly confuse some of the planes overhead. If it were known at home what we were up to, as we said then, there would have been holy murder.

I was alone in another and very real sense. My two older brothers who had been attending the same school and travelled with me each day, at Intermediate level, both decided not to go any further with schooling, but to learn a trade and become bread-winners. The older of the two created a huge disappointment for my parents because he had shown some aspiration towards the priesthood and had been elevated to a high level in their estimation. This was not to be. Even at that early stage it was a devastating blow as he refused point blank to entertain the idea that he might have a vocation. Then the eyes, not only of my parents but of all family, were on me. My older sister was talking of joining the convent, but there had to be a priest, my parents would say. In those days pupils, when asked what they'd like to be in life, would frequently reply a priest or a nun. While my older brothers had set their minds on various trades, the younger ones were showing no interest in schooling, other than the bare minimum; and besides my parents could not afford to pay for any more secondary schooling. The three of us who had been to the Dublin school, had drained the resources quite considerably. I was the only hope in their minds and without me ever expressing my opinion, or being asked how I felt about it, it was decided I was to be the priest in the family. I had no one to talk this over with outside of family and there was no point in bringing it up at family level as there was no room afforded for discussion on this matter. A decision had been made and that's the way it was going to be. Life was like that in many ways. One just accepted things because that's the way it was and no one questioned much in those days because in the then post-war years there was not much on offer and you took what was going simply because there was nowhere else to go. It was exactly in that context that I was presented with a career mapped out for me, signed, sealed and delivered. I felt isolated and alone battling a lonely furrow at this tender age and with a certain element of fear of perhaps upsetting the peace and calm at home, and maybe being the cause of suffering. In a large family situation, if one person was the cause of a shindig, all the others suffered as a result, and the culprit became a target of scorn. I decided to let things float for the moment and perhaps time would solve a lot of things and deep down in myself I began some direct and fervent prayer to God, who I thought might be using this whole process as a means of revealing a vocation to me. I kept saying to myself......we'll see.....maybe....is this the way it comes....I don't know....priests are intelligent...I'm not.....maybe I'll fail....that'll be the proof....kept back in third class?....I'm not intelligent, my father had said....don't tell anyone..... they'll laugh....things are bad enough..... "culchie priest"....keep your mouth shut....I'll show them all....if only a little clarity...what the hell....well shag all this for a lark....become an altar boy......that might give some insight. Days and nights I tossed around in such thoughts. Unknown to myself, I had been enlisted to be an altar boy at the parish church. And off I went again..... silently shouting at those who were organizing my whole life....kick back....no there'll be a row....stand up and speak.....too shy....what do I say.....do what you're told...why me....look at the others...they're free. Stop all this nonsense...... learn your Latin...... for Mass.....you'll be up there on the altar....... become the priests' pal........ you'll have a lovely red soutane..... white surplice. I decided once again to knuckle down as best I could to all that was now beginning to unfold and to look at the exams as they came my way as indications of whether this is what God wanted for me. If I failed any major and necessary exam, then that would be the means of conveying the message to me, obviously failure was a negative indication and passing meant, I was to carry on and explore further. That was the line I took.

The practice of the Catholic faith was very strong in Ireland at that time and any statement made by bishop or priest was taken as gospel and no one even questioned it. As a young boy then,

I got the clear impression that people were still enjoying a sort of religious emancipation. Often the period of persecution was recalled and some were heard to say, "Let's enjoy what we have, to the full." I felt at the time, it was all a mechanical kind of religious practice and it's hard to believe I had these thoughts at the time, but could not express myself, as now. So who was I to say we've too much religion. The demands, rules and regulations, the do's and the don'ts, were being piled on, and no one said a word. We had to go to Mass on Sundays, sometimes more than once. There were many church devotions and novenas, such as: Miraculous Medal devotions on a Monday night, novenas to a variety of saints, sodalities, separate for men and women, rosaries and benedictions, and of course the May and Corpus Christi processions. As the senior altar boy, I had more than my share, being listed to serve at this that and the other. I thought my parents were religious fanatics being under pressure with all of this religious practice. The person who didn't attend was the odd one out. Then perhaps after a long session in the church, the Rosary and all the family trimming prayers were rigidly adhered to on returning home.

Our family Mass on Sunday was usually 8 am Fasting from midnight, was the accepted rule, not even a drop of water could be consumed. I was often weak with the hunger. I even fainted once on the altar. A memory for me at this early morning Mass, was, when a certain lady in the congregation got a fit in the middle of the packed church and she screaming and the sight of her being carried out frothing from the mouth really frightened me, because I felt it was like a demon type of presence in her.

I often wondered if my father had a problem trying to decide whether politics or religion was the most important in his life. He was deeply involved at election time, literally covered from head to toe with election stickers and badges. He was available on the polling day from opening to closing time with his horse and trap to ferry people to the polling stations, provided of course they were the "up Dev" people and guaranteed him they'd vote F.F. His interest in politics stemmed from his own background in the old I.R.A., his military prison sentence, his R.I.C. service, being a founder member of the Garda Siochana, and being stationed in Listowel formerly an R.I.C. barracks where the famous Listowel "mutiny" took place. He could see a way forward and opportunities for Ireland like there never were before. He was very involved in promoting his party's candidates and became acquainted with lots of influential politicians. Some of them tried to encourage him into active politics and go for election, but he backed off and would not accept.

He continued to be very much committed to his little farm and I often walked with him as he turned the sod with the two big horses pulling and puffing under the strain of the single furrow plough. I often had to run all the way to the village to get his five Woodbines in a paper packet and when I'd return, he'd sit back on the headland taking for himself and the horses a well deserved break and saying as he puffed away, "The very thing the doctor ordered." The doctor wouldn't say that today! I delighted, as did the other members of the family, in doing things that pleased people especially the parents, because that always created a pleasing and happy atmosphere. The opposite would have us all scurrying for shelter. When word was out that "The auld chap was on the war path," the place would be like a deserted village in a western cowboy film when a shoot out was about to take place. The name of the wanted or the guilty one, would echo over the place and then those not being on the danger list, would emerge and carry on as usual.

### *Life goes on*
Parish life in Celbridge was typical of any country village those years. Church attendance was a must for everyone, and if you weren't there, you'd be missed and it would be commented upon. One elderly priest, after being in the confession box for a long period would get severe pains in his knees, and while crossing one leg over the other for relief, a

roar could be heard all over the church, "oh....that's terrible.....". The unfortunate leaving the box at that precise moment would emerge red faced. People had a simple and genuine faith but were totally controlled by the power of the church in those years and this was accepted as part of life. There is no doubt that this power was abused by many bishops and priests. Education was lacking for the vast majority in the post war years but when it became free and available for everyone and with the advent of Vatican 11, then Church, State, in fact society in general, was in for revolutionary changes. There was little or no lay involvement in the running of the parish, just attendance at the church ceremonies. I realized elements of scrupulosity, superstition, and often the multiplicity of three in reciting prayers, and this resulted in a mechanical routine of reciting prayers with no real commitment to what was being said. That changed to a large extent over the years to come.

School was going reasonably well and I was using that as another possible means of conveying to me a positive or maybe negative indication in my quest for direction regarding my vocation. I think the fact that I worked so hard to try and pass my Intermediate Certificate should have made it clear enough that I really did wish not only to pass but to do as well as I could. Among the usual required subjects, Latin was one of them, and strangely enough I actually liked that subject, and thought it had a curious sort of mystique about it. I realized the wide significance of Latin, that, although it was a dead language in itself, it was in fact the basis and root of many European Languages, especially, Italian, Spanish, French, and to a certain extent influenced the Celtic and Gaelic language and culture. In a way I was oblivious to its importance in the Church and the studies of Philosophy and Theology. The Mass itself and most other liturgies were all in Latin. So there was an underlying simmering growth going on that was a gentle gradual formation in mind, education and spirit, I was unaware of it at the time. I was in a cloudy mist in my thinking; I was looking no further than my nose. I had not yet heard the phrase, "The Lord works in mysterious ways." I was a seed in a thick pod, waiting to be sown in favourable ground, to take root and blossom forth. Right there and then, the Lord was working and developing in the deep unconscious.

Being in Intermediate Certificate class (now known as Junior Certificate) various vocations promoters would call to our class wondering if there were any possible candidates for the priesthood. Two jet black African priests spoke to us one day and this was now the early fifties about their needs for missionaries and finished by saying that someday we might have an African Mission to Ireland. His words ring in my ear today, when we see the lack of vocations in Ireland while they're flourishing in many third world countries and in Africa. I never had at anytime the least inclination to join a missionary order. Another promoter spoke to us and he was head Army Chaplain, but also had the task of seeking possible candidates for the Dublin scene. He impressed me with his kind and encouraging words and without saying anything, I took his calling card and thought to myself if and when I was really deciding to seriously take steps towards priesthood, then I would like to hear more from him. It was to be a couple of years before I'd make contact with him. A definite and specific seed had been sown here and it made me think. For the first time on my own initiative, I began to pray in my own personal way about all of this.

It was a great sense of joy and achievement to pass the Intermediate Certificate. This gave me a certain boost in self confidence and quite a little pride for the family sake. But there were two elements taking hold on my life at this stage which I did not realize. One was the accepting of the "people pleasing syndrome" as part of life and not being able to see above and beyond it. This is a behavior I adopted as did others just to survive in our family. I probably did not get the love I thought I deserved and may not have been given permission to please myself, to trust myself and to choose a course of action that demonstrated self-trust. All I required was there when needed but not always available at the precise moment of need. The second element taking root without my realizing it was, without getting sentimental, or emotional, not to mention romantic, I needed to convince myself that I was lovable and to keep on telling myself that until I believed it. The seeds of these problematic areas of my life were being sown about this time and I suppose I have to say, it was to take me most of a life-time to learn how to cope with them.

Not surprisingly, considering the hectic year that it was, I got the shingles. This, I was told, was a sign of being run down and emerged from the nervous system. My whole body was covered in sores and our doctor called every day to apply ointment and powder but to no avail. For two whole weeks I did not sleep, day or night. I had been told if this rash spreads and meets from both sides at the back, that was it, I was a "gonner." I spent hours having a look at myself in the mirror, trying to see how close it was getting. All of this worry made me worse. An old farmer friend of the family visited our house every second Friday night for years and when he inquired where I was, the parents told him I was in bed with the shingles. "And did ye not cure him?" he asked. They explained how the doctor had been treating me for two weeks without any improvement. Then he spoke of an old cure he knew of from his own parents. He told them to get a hen from the shed, which everyone thought very strange. But nothing compared with what was to follow. He arrived with the hen and a whole brigade of the family came into my room. He told me he had the cure for me. I was desperate at this stage. He pulled the hen's neck which was the usual method of killing fowl, took his penknife out and cut open its body allowing the blood to flow. He then immediately spread the fresh hot blood all over my body making signs of the cross with it as he went. He told me I wouldn't have to suffer much longer. The scene in the room was like a butcher's abattoir with blood and feathers all over the bed and room. My mother, I can see her now, stood there with the tattered lifeless hen in her hand and said to the man, "What'll I do with the hen?" "Put her in the pot and ate her," was the answer she got. That Friday night was the first sleep I got in two weeks and by Monday morning all the sores had fallen off my body completely, with nothing but a little redness remaining. I learned that this very old cure had been used for many years in Ireland.

I was at this stage taking fiddle lessons on Saturdays from a nun at the infant school where I started. I would travel the one mile journey on my bike with the fiddle box tied to the back. Local kids jeered a bit at me, saying ,"There he goes with his piana on his bike." Early learning of this instrument is slow and painful, but made more so by the fact that the nun with a springy little twig, constantly hit me on the tip of the finger for playing a wrong note. After every lesson, all the knuckles of each hand were red and sore. I really wanted to learn and I was doing quite well, moving up in grades, but apart from every Saturday afternoon being taken up, when I would much rather be out through the fields, I resented the method used and the treatment meted out by this nun. Between this and the memories of my earlier days at this school, no wonder I grew up with a dislike for certain nuns, and many of those I met in later years did not help to change or improve my feelings towards them.

Sometimes my mother asked me to bring home little messages while I was in the village. The one item I had one Saturday was a small quarter packet of tea. The nun told me to put it in the box with the fiddle in case I'd lose it. That was a good idea, and off I went. On arrival and departure, the nun would always unpack and repack the fiddle herself very carefully. As usual the following Saturday, as she unpacked the instrument, she asked if I'd practiced, "Of course Sister, several times," I said. When she opened the case, there was the quarter of tea, sitting as she had left it. A big row followed because I'd told a lie and I had not even opened the case since the last lesson. We parted on very bad terms that day, and I never returned. I did attempt at different intervals later to return to playing the fiddle, with a mixture of success and failure, but the efforts were not sustained. From experimenting with piano, accordion, mouth organ, I stayed with the guitar for a good number of years and got more satisfaction from that than any other instrument.

***Family activities***

Our next door neighbour was in the greyhound business, training, racing and coursing. One of my brothers worked there for a while and learned a good deal about how it all worked. His job was feeding, grooming and walking out the dogs. There were several hundred in all. He was not alone naturally, the walking out of all dogs every day was a must. The rule from the boss was that the one walking could not return until every single dog had emptied their bowels. Sometimes this could take quite a long time and therefore entail an extremely long walk. Between the other workers and my brother, they discovered that by putting a piece of straw up the dogs' posterior, this tickled the back passage and forced the dog into fulfilling the required obligation. It was an unusual picture to see a couple of fellows with about twenty dogs each, all with straws hanging from under their tails. This method enabled them to shorten their walking task quite considerably. Interest in greyhounds came to our place and my father invested, as he did in the machinery, in a pack of, what he called "sooners", meaning the sooner you got rid of them the better. But he did hit on some good winners and made quite a bit of profit on them. They were never kept for long. As soon as they had won a race or two and showed promise, they were sold for a modest profit. Coursing and catching hares was good outdoor fun and excitement. It was for us a great way of enjoying an afternoon and this was by no means cruel to either the dog or the hare. The greyhound track racing was totally different. I often went in the van to help look after our runners while waiting for the race. I learned a good deal about the mechanics of it all. When allowed to watch one of our dogs run one night, I happened to see a six penny piece on the stand floor. I put my foot on it, and didn't move for ages in case someone came to claim it. Eventually I pretended to tie my shoe lace and picked it up. Without saying anything to anyone, I sneaked on a bet with the bookie at a good price and got six shillings back. This was a great thrill and only on the way home did I tell the company about my good fortune.

Sometimes after returning from a race night, a card game would follow in our house. At first it was the simple family game when we'd all be able and allowed to take part. But then the serious stuff started when those with big money got down to poker. The most memorable game was one night when my brother won the huge sum of £30 from a visitor; that cleaned him out. He then put the keys of his car on the table and my brother won that. We were all around the table, including the parents, with mouths wide open. My father, who did not play poker, intervened and told our lad to give the man back his keys and £30, which he did. But the visitor said he would accept them on one condition, that the game should continue. It did, and the brother won the lot back again. He also returned everything for the second time, but the visitor made a deal that he would donate a calf which he had out in his van. My father asked if it was a "white head," these were the valuable type. He said it was. "Don't bother coming out in the cold" he said, "I'll leave it in the shed." First thing next morning my father went out to see the animal and what a shock he got to see a totally white calf. Well, what a con job this was. A totally white calf did not have near the same value as a black or red with a white head. Who won and who lost?

The little shop was doing well and a secondary school which opened across the road, added to the business. I tried my hand at serving a customer once myself. He was a new neighbour, from Portaferry away up North, who spoke with an extreme Northern accent, very quickly, and also had a serious lisp in his speech. Put all that together and it was next to impossible to figure out what he was saying. He ordered something from me and I proceeded to weigh out some potatoes. The man started laughing in hysterics. He had actually asked me for a newspaper.

Some of my older brothers now had girlfriends and would often come in late at night from a date or a dance. A few of them would arrive home together in the van, switch off the engine at the gate and push it the rest of the way. A couple of us would have a trap set for them which was some biscuit tins piled outside the parents' door which they had to pass. A black thread was in place across the corridor to insure the desired would happen. The excitement we younger ones felt waiting for the crash at two o'clock in the morning was breathtaking. With their shoes off for safety sneaking downs the corridor, the crash would come and all hell would break loose, with my father rushing out shouting, "What the hell is goin' on here, where are yuse lot goin' at this hour o' the night?" These kind of happenings are great fun memories.

I loved going to auctions with my father to buy his secondhand furniture, and it's there I learned my bit about antiques. He would say to me when the bidding was going on, "Sit there and don't open your mouth, don't even scratch your nose, that could cost me money." They all had their own little signs as a way of bidding, and the hammer would come down and I'd hardly see a hand move. Outside the furniture shop in the village, the Parish Priest, and my father would sit, often for hours, smoke, chat and solve all the problems of the country.

### *The maturing family*

I often thought our family needed someone like a manager and director of operations, as there was so much happening on all fronts. Outside advisers were often consulted, people like the family doctor, the Parish Priest, (of course he was infallible), or the local T.D. Once the Minister for Agriculture visited us and on getting into his big chauffeur driven car outside the gate, a well-known local lady who was forever peering out her window and missed nothing, was on alert as usual soaking up every aspect of our VIP's visit. Just before entering his car he asked my father what the locality was called. My father aware of the piercing eyes from above almost burning into his back but pretending not to notice, answered in a very loud voice in order to give our inquisitive observer sound as well as vision said, "This whole area is known as the valley of squinting windows."

Letter writing was encouraged at home, and we were all obliged to write to a certain mysterious aunt, my mother's sister, a nun in New York. We had never met her, until her first visit in the mid-fifties. We often wrote letters to non-existent people just for practice, or even to one another in the house. Letters from the parents to get off school were carefully drafted, as were applying for jobs, or making application for apprenticeship places. There was a sense of team work in letter writing.

By the time we had reached our teenage years the biggest shed which was normally full of hay was packed with second-hand furniture. We often thought it was a lot of rubbish, only fit for burning, but the motto and stock answer was always, "It will be worth something some day." We had no idea, that in fact a great number of items, were valuable antiques, which today would be worth a fortune. The big fear among householders in buying secondhand furniture, was woodworm, not only would such infestation destroy the piece itself, but also bring destruction to their homes. Sales took place in the yard as well as the shop in the village. One lady challenged my father on his claim that there was no woodworm in a particular wardrobe. "In fact" she said, "I've found not one but two worm holes in it." The answer she got was, "Well Maam, he went in that hole and out that hole, now he's gone." I'll have to admit, on a few occasions he used the old camouflage of the brown shoe polish, and it worked wonders. The milking cows were on their way out and the farmyard was becoming more like the "You name it we have it" type of place. It looked more like a scrap yard. A man asked my father one day, "What's for sale around here?" the answer he got was, "Everything, including my shirt!" An old eccentric retired doctor often visited just to look around. Winter and summer, he always wore a big heavy crombie overcoat, and on a sweltering hot summer's day with this coat on, I asked him why he wore it, he said, "What keeps out the cold, keeps out the heat."

Everything was secondhand, from the furniture, to the cars, tractors, machinery, and most things were well worn and aged. I loved being around the whole atmosphere in the yard and enjoyed mucking about with the machinery, wanting to have a go at driving the tractor. With such old and often worn out equipment, we often spent a whole day trying to start the tractor or to get a piece of machinery working properly. A breakdown out in the fields, or trying to get a spare part, and fit it, would cost more in time and energy than it was worth. Hours of maintenance far out-numbered actual working or operating hours.

My eldest brother now had his first car, a Baby Austin, better known as "The Matchbox." He was very proud of that car. We were not even allowed to touch it. As an aspiring carpenter, he had his own workshop which was a converted horse box and sometimes while he was in there, a few of us would try to get a sneaky preview of his work by peeping in the window, tease him with annoying little quips, "Are ya all right in there....are ya cold....are ya lonely...what are ya makin'....can we have a drive in yer matchbox car....are ya after hittin' yer finger with the hammer?" He would eventually explode and say, "Go away ya little brats or I'll bevelize yus all." With that he made a burst for the door and we scattered. One day I was a bit slow and last to make it to the corner, whereupon I felt the actual breeze of a big hammer whisk past my ear, missing by about half an inch. If this had been slightly more to one side, I was dead. Such was the anger we had provoked by our teasing. Still I was privileged later to be brought on a holiday in the little Baby Austin, all the way to a place called Grange Con in Co. Wicklow, to stay with an old aunt of ours. The journey which would take about forty minutes in a modern car of today, took us two and a half hours. It was night time when we arrived and before retiring to my bed in the attic, my aunt wished to have a little drive in this most modern car. The small battery gave barely adequate lighting, and being a warm summer's night, there were lots of flies and moths in the air. As we bounced along the narrow bumpy road, the old lady, fascinated by this fast and very high tech machine, asked the driver a very observant question, "What sort of oil, or is it carbide, do you burn in the lamps?" My brother, greatly amused by the question, urged her on a bit, "Why do you ask that, auntie?" Well she said, "There's an awful lot o' sparks cumin' out o' them."

My brother had made a decision to sell this little gem, but one morning as he was emerging from the back gate to venture out on to the highway to the big city, the front wheels failed to respond to the instructions from the steering wheel to go right, and instead, went straight across the road ending up nose down in the ditch. A very angry and disappointed brother stormed out of the car, abandoned it as it was, and got a lift from a passing car. No one dared to go near it, for fear of making a bad situation worse. He recovered his "little baby" that evening himself, got it cleaned up, painted it by brush in a nice bright blue and I was standing by watching and listening as the deal was being struck. It was a drizzling rainy afternoon and the prospective buyer asked if the wipers worked, presuming them to be motor driven, "Oh, yes they work," was the answer, as my brother quickly reached in the driver's door to the knob above the windscreen. While the man was examining the back area, my brother gave it a few twists which was in fact the only means of moving the wiper blade, in that way clearing the mist off the glass. He was really chuffed with himself by his own quick and sharp intuition. He was sad and I can tell you, I was very sad, to see and hear two hands smack as all of £30 was handed over for the little "Matchbox" I had grown to love.

The older half of the family was now fanning out, in apprenticeships, starting little jobs, learning a trade locally, one taking to the farm, and at first this last one did not like the farm because it was not different enough; it was not away from home, it had no real future he felt, it was not a trade like the others. He was expected to be up early and feed all the animals before he was allowed to have his breakfast, but he was not a good riser and the same brother rolled a lot in his sleep. One night he rolled right out of the bed onto the floor, over to the far wall, proceeded to roll back the opposite way and continued right under the bed complete with all the bed clothes; he was nearly declared missing or absconded. But to overcome his early morning work before breakfast, he developed an ingenious plan. He would get out the bedroom window, the house was single storey, grab a bucket, walk straight into the kitchen as if he'd been out so busy feeding and tending that he forgot to leave the bucket down. He would be welcomed by my father already tucking into his own big fry-up, saying, "Is everything fed and okay out there?" "Sure, all is well," would be the answer. "Good man, sit down there now and have a good feed, you deserve it after all that hard work."

If I was willing to get up earlier, a lift was available in a Ford Poplar which a brother drove to his place of apprenticeship. I'd get one shout. "If you want to come with me, I'm going now," and if I didn't respond promptly, I missed the lift and had to bus it. I was beginning to try my hand at smoking the odd fag, just to get the feel of what it was like. All the older ones, including my sister, were smoking by now, and secretively at that. But my brother driving the Ford to town knew quite well that I was dabbling in the nicotine world and eventually gave me one on the way saying, " Here, you don't have to keep it a secret from me, I know you're at it." Mind you that gave me a great incentive to be on time for my morning lift, which now included a free fag and an uninhibited smoke.

Near the school there was a lovely old lady with a sweets stall and all of us got to know her very well. She knew many names and often missed certain lads if they were away for any length of time. Old pennies was our usual currency, and we'd have very few of them. She also unofficially had available for "regular customers" single cigarettes at 1d. each. There were quite a few experimenting with the smoking lure. It was a very serious breach of rules, if caught smoking in the school grounds or buildings. Each day after school there was always a big gathering around the little three wheeled basket trolley. Business was brisk and in addition to the sweets being passed around, the smokes could be filtered too, without detection.

I had a huge dilemma on my hands. I was able to save one penny if I walked the three mile journey to the point of connection for my home bus, which was Capel St. bridge and on certain days I could make it on time by walking, because we sometimes got off a little earlier than usual. The real problem (and this is something I've never spoken of) was what to spend my money on. There were three separate things on which I could spend the penny, (the toilet wasn't one of them) a penny bought five of my favourite sweets, the honey bee. Secondly, it could buy a fag for the auld smoke, but thirdly and quite remarkably I loved to drop into a little church just down the road on my way, to say a prayer and light a candle which cost 1d. I was often torn apart trying to make a decision on this. The odd time I'd walk three days, save 3d. and had the pleasure of all three desires on the one day. That was rare. But the days I'd have the sweets or the other days when I'd go for the fag, were never near as rewarding as the days I'd go to the Church to pray and light the candle. Occasionally after satisfying the body rather than the soul, I would sometimes go the church anyway, say the prayer and express sorrow that I'd no penny to light the candle, and I'd have a certain element of guilt. The days when I'd sacrifice the sweets or the fag for the candle, were days of great inner peace and tranquillity accompanied by a huge sense of strength in a type of victory I'd won.

### *My two sisters*
The ratio of eight boys to two girls seemed a bit off balance but in fact it worked out over the years without any major problems. The older was fifth from the top leaving her my

immediate senior and therefore chores inside and outside came to us both very often. Anyway she always wished to be out and about with the lads, and not intending any disrespect to her, she delighted in being "a tomboy." She was literally into everything that the boys were up to about the place and when it came to going to the pictures and, later, dances, she was first into the van. She was fun-loving and always full of the joys of life. She would try everything that was on offer and never missed a trick. Leaving school after Primary Certificate, she worked in the little shop at home in its opening years, but never intended to stay there any longer than she had to. Living life to the full, she was an early smoker, had a boyfriend, was the cause for concern when out late, and all of that. Then to everyone's surprise and quite dramatically, she returned an engagement ring to an intended suitor, and went off to join an order of nuns. Finding it difficult to return to books and study, she made the grade, was professed and worked in England and then went on to South America for some years. She did quite well for about ten years but did not find fulfilment in that life, left the order and became a Spanish and Portuguese interpreter. Eventually she settled and married in Canada, where she and her husband, both retired, now live.

My younger sister, who was second youngest, was of a very different character and temperament. I suppose it would be true to say, she took after my mother, while the older took after my father. This younger sister also left school after primary and also took up working in the little shop, now well established. She was of a more quiet nature, reserved and studious in manner. Staying very close to my mother, and with little interest in the outdoor or social activities, she became what we might call, a home bird. She was a great worker and extremely helpful in every way to my mother, who at this stage was beginning to slow down a bit and most certainly needed constant help around the house, especially with the shop on top of everything. With most of the gang still living at home, even though the house had been extended and modernized somewhat, it was a lot of work even for two, full time at it. It was this younger sister's own choice to spend these years devoted to helping, supporting, very often replacing the now ageing and tiring mother, despite regular luring from other members to get out socially, she was determined to fulfil a very needy and necessary role in the home. It was no great surprise to anyone, when she too joined the same order of nuns as my older sister, and went through the same difficult task of getting back to books and study. She too made the required grade, was professed, worked in England for a number of years, and then went on to South America, and now twenty years later, she continues happily and successfully with her missionary work in that part of the world.

## CHAPTER THREE

## FUTURE TAKING SHAPE

The couple of years leading into the Leaving Certificate passed very quickly and looking at some areas of life as it was then, such as school, family, parish, and also my own feelings and attitudes, it seemed to me that these might remain as they were forever. Everyone was busy doing things and helping to contribute to the needs and welfare of the growing and more demanding family. The urge to earn and help put the bread and butter on the table was in the air at home and in the country at large. In the nineteen fifties our nation began to show promising economic growth and all out efforts were being made by the politicians of the day to take Ireland to a new and exciting level of independence. The post war depression and huge emigration rate of the fifties painted a dull picture at the time, but the foresight and sheer Irish grit of so many people in the political, social, economic and religious fields, gave people hope, and the type of attitude and motto we'd grown to learn at home to try and get into business of our own and this was very much part of the growing spirit becoming evident nationwide. More than just the few educated people were beginning to appear and many were now able to stand on their own two feet and not have to run to church people, or local professional personnel to sort out their problems. So in the late fifties and early sixties we saw the beginning of a dissolving of church power and the state having an increasing power over people in our society. Independence was looming and new political parties were being formed, Vatican 11 was beginning to be implemented.

Our home was not a place of celebrating any of the usual events such as birthdays, exam or career successes, because everyone was literally too busy to waste time and hard earned money on anything that might be regarded as superfluous in nature. So birthday parties, even if they were twenty firsts were not celebrated. It meant we grew up not even knowing our birthdays were slipping by. How things have changed in the year 2000. When I read of parents spending £10,000 on a child's first birthday party, the mind boggles.

My own day-today life settled into a routine. While I felt somewhat guilty for not actually being a bread winner, but rather a drag on the system, I got the distinct message that everyone at home was comfortable with that. Personally I felt quite left out of many things that were going on, still that's the way it was to be. The battle of the sweets, the fag and the church/prayer/candle continued but with a difference now, in that, I found myself praying not just for help in making a decision as to whether I should or shouldn't go on to be the priest, but rather praying for help to be a priest. The church/candle routine had more victories on record in these latter years leading up to the Leaving Certificate and final year in Secondary School. It was to be the culmination of eleven years of monotonous daily bus travel. Twice in that time I had to walk the entire journey home, due to fog on one occasion and snow on another. Sore feet and aching limbs needed nursing on arrival.

The big Leaving Certificate exam finally came and strangely enough I was quite relaxed and even quietly confident. Just my luck that there was a national scandal that year. We were nearly finished the examination with one paper left to sit, when it was discovered that a large number of the question papers had been leaked out to pupils before the exam, so the papers already completed were now declared void and were scrapped. It was the first time the papers had been printed in Ireland, rather than in Holland, and some smart printer thought that this would be a quick way of making some money. All of this led to a huge outcry on the part of all the pupils nationwide. We had to sit the entire exam again, answering badly printed question papers which were rushed out to try and save what could have become a sheer mockery. Despite all the upset, I passed and had the necessary grades for matriculation and entry to university.

I declared myself, in what I thought was a clear and independent decision, as being interested in the Dublin Diocese. That was helped by a couple of visits to the Army Chaplain who had come to our school some years earlier. I wrote personally to the President of the Diocesan Seminary for an interview. This had to be heralded by a recommendation from our local Parish Priest, who of course gave a glowing reference of this marvellous young man who hailed from such excellent parents and family. This ageing priest had great experience to his credit, having been an Army Chaplain himself for many years. He was also the founder of the Dublin boxing stadium. In his letter, he attributed to me such admirable qualities, that my ego received a superb boost, and as I looked at myself in the mirror and reflected on the qualities seen in me by such a knowledgeable man, I thought to myself, I'm not such a "gobdaw" after all.

As I grew up, the "pleasing people" syndrome was ingrained in me coming from family and society at the time. The emotional and psychological craving to be loved, were part of my make-up, and I had this very sincere and genuine urge to try and do things for other people. Many well intentioned advisers tried to tutor me on what would be the best and most acceptable answers at the interview. My gut feelings immediately reacted to this well intended advice because this was not some ordinary job I was going for, but rather trying to answer a possible call of a vocation to a special ministry in the Church. Delighted that I was actually called for interview at all, I made a very clear and independent decision to follow my own instincts. In my thinking there was no room for an artificial or concocted approach.

I was given a lift in the Ford Poplar into a demesne the likes of which I'd never seen before, the long drive up the avenue, the huge buildings, and then the imposing stone steps up to the front door. The President gave me as warm a welcome as he would allow himself to give. He did not meet me at the door of his office, but sat from beginning to end behind his large mahogany desk. I was to discover later that the man had only one leg, resulting from a car accident he had some years previous. He got around when he so wished with the aid of a stick and an artificial leg, he could also drive his own specially equipped car. He kept his questions simple and clear and maintained a sort of cold indifferent front. That's the way these fellows were made, I thought. The questions were mostly about home life, school, attitude to parents, authority, teachers and fellow pupils. Having been to a day school how I'd regard the boarding situation in college, and so on. Then the final and most important question was, "Why do you wish to become a priest?" I can remember my answer very clearly, "I would like to be in a position where I could help people." These were my exact words. The meeting ended with the usual, "Thank you, and I'll be in touch." It was a few weeks later when I got the word that I had been accepted and was to enter the college in October of that year, 1957.

While most of my seeking clear indications along the way, was through things like exams, or some personal sense of communication with God, I was still full of doubt, unsure, certainly nervous, fearful and then the thinking out loud started again: …what if I don't like it….maybe very unhappy…..I'm going to be lonely…..miss the family, home life, the fields, the machinery, furniture…..all these other fellas……my God……. total strangers….the food….inside the walls until Christmas…….do we even get home then?….I don't know.

Many sleepless nights followed and the three things that kept me going were, faith, family and friends. I was concerned about the expense I was putting the family to, not only for the clothes and outfits we needed, but also all the fees necessary for the seminary and university. I was relieved when I heard a society called St. Joseph's Young Priests Society kindly agreed to give financial backing, and so that took some of the burden off the family.

The day of arrival was traumatic for me because I thought how much easier it was for those who had been to boarding schools and were used to the idea of being away from home. Anyway I made up my mind to try and knuckle down as best I could and realize that this was the beginning of the break away from home and that life was never going to be the same again. Within twelve months of me going to the seminary, three other members of the family were to venture out into the deep. My younger sister entered the convent, and two brothers married. So I was not alone in leaving home, and the fact that I knew these other members were moving on, was a consolation in itself.

### *Seminary days*

Rather than give an in-depth detailed account of seminary life in Clonliffe and Maynooth during the fifties and sixties, I'd like to stand back and take a wider and somewhat light-hearted look at this period in my life and how some events, memories and occasions stand out in my reminiscing. May I add also that I will record events exactly as they happened, including the language and expressions used on the occasions, otherwise they would not convey the true reality and therefore lose their authenticity. Apart from the imposing buildings and extensive grounds, aspects such as staff, rules of the house, accommodation, food, sport, hobbies, pastimes, likes and dislikes, and many such things are always an easy way of leading a group of past pupils into a fun-filled conversation on each one's personal experiences and involvement in memorable events.

I first entered Dublin's Diocesan Seminary, Clonliffe College, early October 1957 as part of a group of thirty students, mostly from County Dublin and the nearby counties of Kildare, Meath, Westmeath, and a few from further West and North west. Some of these would have been to junior seminaries and boarding colleges, and so for them coming to a live-in situation was nothing strange or very much different, but for the vast majority, including myself, it was a totally new beginning and a somewhat daunting experience. Watching them all arrive, presented some interesting viewing, in the variety of shapes and sizes: tall ones, small ones, fat ones, thin ones, huge luggage, little luggage, (I had a big old fashioned trunk like the one you'd see on the back of an American stagecoach) but all of us with no small apprehension, as together we ventured into the unknown and, perhaps for many, a trying and experimental period in our lives. Within an hour we were assembled by the Dean and given some immediate instructions printed on a sheet of paper to be studied carefully, followed by a tour of the building indicating services and places we needed to know, and we were told that the strict rules and regulations would be imposed and as from 8pm that very evening. We only had a couple of hours of real freedom in which to unpack and familiarize ourselves with faces and places.

The early morning ringing of the rising bell was to become part of life for the next seven years, followed by prayers, Mass, breakfast, recreation, and then the work of the day. On this very first morning, one student was packing to leave; for him it was a bed and breakfast stay. He was a keen fiddle enthusiast, and when he was told by the prefect on his floor that he was not allowed to play his instrument at 2am in the morning, he decided the place was not for him, and so with all his newly acquired gear he was heading back out into the world. Within a couple of days we were launched into something nobody expected, the thirty days retreat, given by the Jesuit Order. This was a whole month of total and absolute silence, day and night, with religious exercises of all sorts, totally foreign to us.

The only form of recreation was the entire group doing some gardening on the front drive, weeding scuffling etc. an easy and cheap way of getting the borders cleaned up. We were watched by the dean of discipline or the president himself from a top window with the aid of binoculars, to ensure nobody was talking or fool-acting and if so, they were severely reprimanded. I really felt like an inmate of a high-security prison. This month of testing and sorting quickly brought quite a number of students to a decision, that this life was not for them, and they left. It put many others on the edge of their searching, but some made up their minds to give it a go for at least one year in fairness to themselves, family and all concerned. By the end of our first year, ten had left, leaving us with the round figure of twenty. That figure was to hold for most of the seven year study course, and we finally had seventeen ordained. We had been told by the more experienced ones ahead of us, that those who survived the thirty days retreat, had a good chance of running the full course.

But the strict discipline continued relentlessly. Apart from the written rules of the house, individuals were quickly informed to correct any personal defective characteristics which they may have had, such as the way they walked, talked, laughed, general decorum, and in some cases if a student was over weight, to reduce it within a certain time scale. I was red-carpeted by the president for eating my boiled egg with the spoon in my left hand. I was what we call a "cittogue." On entering the president's office, the caller had to face traffic lights. Red meant, "occupied," orange "wait," and green "enter." If two students were seen walking out together more than twice in one week, this was regarded as a special friendship, and not allowed. All outdoor and indoor activities were closely observed. During meals in the refectory, the dean or president, would walk around the room for the duration, closely watching every move of every student, while a reader bellowed out some passage of a suitable spiritual book for the day.

For those who wished, and I was one, smoking was allowed outdoors for one half hour of recreation time only and was strictly banned indoors and outside the allotted times. But just as contraband foods, like biscuits, tea, coffee, sweets etc. were all taboo, there were ways and means around these difficult rules. The smoking times were so limited, the farm yard down the back was a regular haunt, and I often felt that some cattle and fowl must have suffered severely from passive smoke inhalation. The smoke, tea or coffee (boiling the water by means of a small emersion heater in a cup), the cake, biscuit, the out-of-hour smoke, always satisfied far more under the pressure of secrecy than when taken in the normal way. I established some friendships and quickly began to realize that a new type of family was being formed as time went on, and that my classmates in a sense replaced my family. The class as such, from the very beginning gelled into a bond of friendships and relationships, that fellows like myself not only needed but were to depend on for survival in future years.

One of my smoking friends complained of a mattress too soft, and I had one, which was too hard. We decided to swap despite the fact that he was on the floor above me, and worse still that we would have to break a cardinal rule of not entering another student's room. A day and a precise time were set to make the swap during a period of the afternoon when very few people were around. Having synchronized our watches, we moved simultaneously, and met mid-way on the stairs each carrying his mattress, almost identical to leaf carrying ants. Both of us realized at a crucial stage of the proceeding that a member of staff was standing on the landing, watching this most mysterious activity unfolding before his eyes. We whispered as we passed each other, to just "act naturally". Everything passed without another word being said by anyone, leaving the member of staff, bewildered and mesmerized as to what was going on. Our loads were deposited in our respective rooms and a rapid departure made by both of us. It was next day before we conferred on the success of our mission but after all the effort, it transpired that mine was now too soft and his was too hard. We had to live with it.

Apart from all the in-house daily routine and spiritual exercises, we also had common chores, such as cleaning bathrooms, toilets, scrubbing and polishing the long corridors, as well as keeping our own rooms, which were very basic, clean and tidy. Some outdoor work, like gardening and general cleaning, was encouraged. Any of the indoor or outdoor duties came fairly natural to me as I had been used to all that sort of work at home. It was not so easy for some who had no such practice. Football and sport fields had to be maintained, and towards the end of the first year, there was an unusual happening when we had what was called "the deacon's race." This was for those in their final year who were about to be ordained, and we being in our first year, looked up to these fellows as if they were gods. It was a fun afternoon of entertainment when these final year guys put on some sort of "mad" event and tried to make it unusual and unique. It was similar to a type of university rag ball or the like. Anyway they all dressed up in funny gear and proceeded to have a game of football in the outfits. In order to create an exciting distraction, one fellow in pretending to run after the ball quite near the Tolka River, continued to the banks and jumped in dressed as he was, and swam across. This was early May and the water was ice cold. He ended up contracting pneumonia and had to have his ordination postponed by a week.

Each Sunday we walked in a large group to the city's Pro-Cathedral for a solemn Mass dressed in full soutanes, collars, and an outer toga, together with a large wide-rimmed Roman hat. We really were a sight to view each Sunday. But people got used to us and soon passed little remark. Down Gardiner St. the kids hounded us for holy pictures and we'd bribe them with lovely ones, so that they in return would run into the shops and get us some contraband supplies. Several times the youngsters would let the cat out of the bag when they'd shout for everyone to hear, including our supervisors, "Father, they've no nut chocolate." We were all called Father because we all looked like priests. But the full company would continue walking, heads and eyes down like monks in a monastery.

With the big retreat now over our next venture was starting in the university and this time we travelled on bikes, which again was a sight for people to behold; this huge crowd of cyclists all dressed in black, wearing hats, proceeding along a fixed route keeping in twos as we went, and like the walking rule, a change of partners had to be followed regularly.

One wet misty morning my partner who wore thick glasses with his head down against the wind and rain, his glasses quite obscured, and listening to me telling him a story which he found very interesting, had his vision so impaired, he had little attention left to devote to where he was going and ended up crashing into a car. Another morning in almost identical circumstances, the same fellow, cycling on my left side, was again so distracted that he did not stay with the rest of us rounding a gradual bend to the right, but instead continued straight on, nearly ending up in the Liffey. I being the cause of these two incidents, received some reprimanding, in language that could only be described as unbecoming to a clerical student.

We were now landed in the middle of a country-wide mix of students, lay, male and female (which added a little colour to the scene), all of whom like us clerical students, were studying Arts. The lecture hall we assembled in held about three hundred and fifty students and it was packed beyond that number. The first university lecturer appeared who was a lay man with a very stern and abrupt manner. He briefly welcomed us to the college, then proceeded to explain that this first year was a vital one for all of us, because only half the number in the room could go on and sit the B.A degree, simply because there was no room to accommodate the numbers in the other lecture halls. He divided the entire room with a gesture of his hand, saying one half will go on, the other half will be out. This was to be decided according to the standard of results from the exam for all at the end of this first year; "So it's up to you," he said, "make up your minds, which half you wish to be in." That set tremendous pressure on all of us from the very start.

There was a mixture of lay and clerical lecturers and professors, and the whole atmosphere and terminology coming across were totally new to me. I was beginning to hear for the first time words like, philosophy, psychology, metaphysics, logic and when the word "schizophrenia" was used in class, it received such an uproar of laughter, that the very serious professor was greatly annoyed at our ignorance and went on to explain what a serious mental illness this was. During a lecture on Roman History one day, most of us clerical students were bundled in one corner of the hall, and one of my class, an ice-cold poker faced trickster, put a billiard ball rolling down the main aisle of the lecture hall, narrowly missing the professor and bouncing off the blackboard wall. He picked on a totally innocent fellow right beside the real culprit, and threw him out of the class.

One of our clerical professors of Metaphysics, was a tall and totally bald man with a whisper-like voice accompanied by a nervous twitchy little cough as he spoke. He was a pleasant and kind man and always had a smile and time for any students who approached him about any matter. One day during lunch break quite a large crowd of students were assembled in the main front hall, and in the middle of them was a dirty looking old dog which would not leave. So the students were endeavoring to remove with shuffling foot gestures and rather subdued use of the words "f...k off out of here," when out of nowhere came our soft speaking, gentle professor, who always walked briskly with a spring in his step, flowing toga and a bundle of lecture notes under his arm, and he happened to see and hear exactly what was going on in the middle of the main hall. So he went over to the circle of students, towering over them all. As he joined the perimeter of the gathering, he said in his usual whisper-like voice, "No, no, no, boys and girls, that's no way to treat that poor little doggie, you should all say, shoo doggie, shoo doggie, and then he'll f...k off himself." He then calmly walked on with his usual springy step without saying another word and left them all gasping in wonder. That same professor was a keen all-year-round swimmer at the famous forty foot, men only spot. His tall bald headed figure was a familiar one at the diving place. He dived in one day and as he did so, his bathing togs slipped to his knees and in his efforts to rectify the potentially embarrassing situation, his posterior appeared above water during the struggle, and his pals watching his battle with the misplaced togs, just said, "Aaah, poor old professor, he must have split his head."

During the summer holidays it was a very strict rule that clerical students wore their full clerical garb and hat at all times while in public. This was a strange and difficult regulation and really cramped the holiday spirit in many ways. I went around a lot on my bike and was often mistaken for a younger brother of mine, who was a barber by trade and in the beginning when he had no fixed premises to work from, he himself went around on his bike with his little bag on the back and called to the homes of his customers to cut their hair. So many people when they'd see me, would think I was the barber and ask me, "When are ya comin' to cut me hair." Despite all the restrictions while in public, and by the way, a report on behaviour had to be sent regularly to the college authorities by the local priests, I enjoyed my usual involvement on the little farm and also took delight and pride in painting and decorating when needed. With constant improvements being made to our house, I was always delighted to muck in and do whatever I had to.

Among some of the unusual jobs I had to do during holiday time, this one stands out in my memory. One of my older brothers and his wife had started a drapery shop in the village and also had a dry cleaning agency included. While I was on summer holiday one year, they asked me to mind the shop for them for two days; they were going to a wedding one day and to a race meeting the second. They told me that being Monday and Tuesday, the shop would not be busy, it would mostly involve taking in clothes for dry cleaning, tagging them and giving the customer a docket. All went well on the Monday, it was mostly customers with cleaners or those buying small items like thread and wool etc. Tuesday was also going smoothly, until in the middle of the afternoon, an elderly lady came in and asked me for a "roll-on." "Pardon me?" I said. "Roll-on," she said, "You know what I mean, corset." I went up the ladder and was looking at the shoes, wondering what the hell I was going to do. I came back down and asked her, "What size?" She gave me some figures and I went up the ladder again looking at the shoes. I decided I had to explain my position to her and told her I was there to take in the cleaners and asked her if she would come back tomorrow when my sister-in-law would get her what she wanted. So the lady did come back the next day, got her item of clothing as requested and as she was leaving asked my sister-in-law, "By the way, who was that fellow you had serving in the shop yesterday, because I asked him for a corset, and he told me to come back tomorrow, they were all gone to the cleaners."

During our first and subsequent years, Archbishop J.C. McQuaid, talked to each and every student personally and in private, on a variety of subjects, all to do with formation for our future ministry. But also, and vitally important to me anyway, he gently and kindly told us how to maintain personal hygiene. All of this was very time-consuming and tedious for him but he always showed great patience and kindness throughout.

I was successful in reaching the B.A. exam which I sat in Earlsfort Terrace now the National Concert Hall. On the first day the girl in front of me was doing a Science paper, and in the first minutes of reading the questions over a couple of times, she fainted right on the floor at my feet. She was carried out and never returned. But with that aside, I went on to pass my B.A. successfully which pleased me very much. It was during this year that debates in the home college were all the go. I never spoke either on a panel or from the floor, until one night, I couldn't resist telling the company of a funny incident that happened that day, and it required me to mimic how another student had acted and spoken earlier. I was thrilled by the laughter and applause I received. That was the first time in my life to date that I realized I could make people laugh. Not knowing at the time, that it was going to stand to me in a big way in a role I was to follow later in life.

I now had reached a transition stage from Philosophy to Theology, and was heading for Maynooth College, the National Seminary, to study the latter. I had a continuous on-going struggle in reconciling all the rules and regulations with what we were supposed to do out there in the world in the near future. The system had us so cut off from reality, I failed to see the connection between our training and the strict disciplinary period of so-called formation. This concern of mine was realized in later life, and I needed to educate myself again in the real world of people, their lives, their faith, their problems and to try and mould myself, whereby I could apply in some practical way what I had taken from the years in seminary.

## *Maynooth Theology*

I was one of six who was asked to go to the National Seminary in Maynooth, to study Theology, beginning in 1960, for four years. This delighted me for a few reasons but mainly because Maynooth was very near to Celbridge. It had six hundred or more students from all over Ireland, including Northern Ireland. It was more country orientated and in many ways had a broader outlook than Clonliffe. So these advantages were a help to me in starting the second phase of my seven year preparation for priestly ministry. It was also something to look forward to in getting a complete new break from what was a very close knit insular situation in the city college. The Maynooth scene was vast which leant itself to a greater sense of freedom, but at the same time it had its own set of seminary rules which were just as strict. I settled there better and quicker than anywhere before and with five of my original class mates with me, it was like bringing part of the family along.

Theology, with its major sections such as: Moral, Dogma, Canon Law, Church History, Scripture, Liturgy, Sociology, now gave a reason for the building of the foundation during the first three years of Philosophy at U.C.D. and Clonliffe. At the time I wondered at the reasons behind some of the subjects, but that was made clear once the study of Theology began. Although strict in their own way, I found the staff at Maynooth a little more friendly and open with students, and this gave me a better sense of maturity and self confidence. Although I was still very shy and quite naïve, I found that public speaking, answering in class or doing oral exams, were still a great challenge. But deep down I had a confidence that "this too shall pass."

There was an indoor swimming pool which was quite basic with little or no heating, just changing rooms around the ground level and also at top level. It was here I first acquired my limited ability to swim, but at least enough to enjoy a jump in the water when I felt like it. The pool was known in the college as "the plunge" because it was the only way to enter. There was an unforgettable and horrifying accident in my time, when a student dived from the top balcony but misjudged the angle of entry, banged his head off the side, and was killed. The sight of his body and the red pool, was a frightening experience. It was quite a while before it was opened again, but when it re-opened a very strict rule was imposed, on penalty of expulsion, not to dive from the top. Within weeks, fellows were plunging from the top again.

Many people ask about the haunted room at the college, with the story of one suicidal jump from this top storey window to his death, and another attempted. The story goes that the first student was literally forced against his will to the window and without knowing what he was doing, had fallen to his death. The room was vacant for a long period, until another student volunteered to try it out, because he was sceptical in relation to the circumstances leading to the death of the first unfortunate student and he wished to find out for himself. He thought the details concluding the evidence in the first case were all very suspect.

He insisted on staying in the room on his own for a night to see if anything would happen. In the early hours of the morning loud cries and a severe struggle could be heard, and others nearby, over heard this and rushed to the room. When they tried the door it was locked, although it was agreed specifically to leave it unlocked. So they quickly broke it open to find this student was in the process of cutting his throat, and only because they intervened and removed the cut throat razor from his hand, he too would have died. He recovered and was lucky to be in a position to actually tell his own story. Apparently he was sleeping soundly until about 2am, and was awoken by some strange force which made him get out bed and reach for his own razor (these were still in use at the time) and then although he was fully conscious, he could not stop his own hand from proceeding to cut his throat. It was as if he was being assaulted, but there was nobody there. He was lucky and certainly less sceptical. The whole front wall of the room was then broken away and a shrine in the entire opening was dedicated to St. Joseph and that's as it remains today.

The studies progressed fairly smoothly with an exam at the end of each year, sometimes oral and other times written. During the year there were spot tests, very often with no fore-warning, and these were in Latin. While most of us knew the material, it was very difficult to express it in Latin. One student attempting to answer a question was really struggling with the

Latin, and he began his answer with, "He knew", which in Latin is "scit" but he pronounced it as "shit". That was the only word he spoke, followed by a long silence and bursting titters from the rest of us, he was told to sit down.

Our Sociology professor who was a prolific writer, was proof reading some of his material for yet another book while we were doing a written exam. As his sheets of typed script kept coming out over the top of his lecture podium, he suddenly burst out laughing. We all downed pens until he told us what was so funny. He had no choice. Apparently in his script he had quoted a scripture passage which should have read, "It is easier for a camel to pass through the eye of a needle than for............" But a misprint of the text read, "It is easier for a camel to piss through the eye of a needle........."

The talent among the students was unbelievable. There were of course the many academics, who were aiming high with various ambitions in their sights and their respective dioceses and bishops had great expectations and hopes for their own men. While there was some inter-diocesan rivalry, it was not of the vicious nature, certainly in the field of study, but perhaps in the field of football, sometimes inter diocesan and inter-county clashes, were fought with great gusto. I was not much into sports, but tried most of the games for the fun of it. I improved my typing by joining the Typing Club, where we had to type out all the lectures for the professors. This took up a lot of recreational time. I also joined the Musical Society and that got me back playing the fiddle. I played seconds in a twenty piece string orchestra. They called me "second fiddle." I practiced this during my free time often to the annoyance of staff and some smart geniuses sometimes threw pennies in my window, but I could never catch the culprits.

While diocesan groups mostly stuck together and all had their own particular meeting spot, there was still good intermingling. In fact I usually sat between two Belfast lads who were friendly but never let me away with anything. There was support from fellow diocesan students and this helped in getting through the four years of study and exams quite smoothly. A lot of food was naturally consumed each day. Like all institutions, monotonous repetition of menus often wore people out. On Sundays and special occasions, a roast of beef or lamb was served at each table of ten. The carving duty went round in rotation and it was a heavy responsibility to insure that all ten got an equal share, and that you had enough left for yourself. That's why over the years past students of Maynooth were always excellent carvers when it came to meat!

The months and years were slipping by and the putting of all this into practice was beginning to loom on the horizon, I still failed to see the thinking behind the confinement and such strict rules. In those years, one could not beat or change the "system" be that Church or State. I had a genuine anxiety of applying the theory in practice and this was justified very quickly. So this application was to be a whole new period of education through sheer experience, and sometimes through trial and error. Some of the more practical lessons came towards the end, like liturgy presentation and preaching techniques. The lecturer in the latter was a sound down to earth man and left a good impression in his training. He insisted on the preacher being brief and to the point and I must say I picked up a lot of tips and increased confidence from him. This man often scolded fellows who were wrapping up a talk or homily and were dragging out the finish too long. He said they were like planes coming in to land, with undercarriage down, but failing to land.

Coming towards the final exams, students had an oral or written option. The system was such that if you passed the oral, you did not have to sit the written. I always found that oral exams were a better test of knowledge, than the written and they (the staff) knew this quite well from their own experience. One History professor used to say to a student if he was not doing too well at the oral, "My good man, I think you should go out and fill your pen." There was a very

AWAKENING

# FAVOURITE THINGS AND PLACES

# AWAKENING

# AWAKENING

# AWAKENING

# A W A K E N I N G

# AWAKENING

# AWAKENING

# AWAKENING

# FAVOURITE THINGS AND PLACES

interesting method when the oral exam for Scripture was scheduled. It took place in an ordinary lecture hall, the three examiners would sit in a row on the ground floor, while the student/examinee, would sit up where the professor would normally lecture from. This left opportunity for a public gallery as it were, behind the examiners, who obviously could not see what was going on, and this public arena consisted of fellow students who were, unknown to the examiners, able to give sign language hints to the unfortunate up on the podium. One most memorable occasion which has been talked about and enjoyed ever since, was when the examiners were waiting for one final and crucial name in an answer. This was often the case, where they would, give us one final date or name, and then you'd be finished. The name from scripture this particular student needed and was trying to remember, was "Papias". All of the prompters in the back gallery were frantically gesticulating with their hands to convey female breasts. The student got the message they were trying to pass to him okay, but the answer he gave to the examiners was, "Didymus."

While going right through seminary life, we had a spiritual director whose task it was to try and shape our lives in a manner that would bring God into our daily thinking to make Him part of all we were endeavoring to do. The director was a visiting priest from the Vincentian Order and not one of the resident staff. I can only speak for myself when I say that at no stage then or in fact even for years after ordination, was I fully satisfied within myself as to the real meaning of a personal God in one's life. I could identify with the people today who acknowledge God "as they understand Him" and I suppose that's fair enough, but to say that I had a special feeling of a Presence within me, would not be true. Naturally I had come on a lot since childhood, but right through the seminary years, I really did expect that all the Philosophy and Theology, would have to in some way give me a much clearer vision and a better conviction, in matters of faith. I thought that God through all this, would make His presence felt and since I was going to do His work through the ministry of the priesthood, that a special relationship with the over-all director of things, would come about.

Pre-conceived ideas of the meaning of "the priest" were still there, and even remained for many years into ministry. I was brought up with the idea that the priest was a highly educated fellow who knew everything there was to know about life, the world, God and all to do with Him. After all, when I was young, so many people turned to the priest seeking answers to all sorts of problems. But right up to the end of the preparations, things were not happening for me as I thought they would. It was interesting to learn recently that the late Cardinal Basil Hume struggled all his life trying to come to terms with how God could possibly love him totally and unconditionally. I thought maybe things would change and having received all the signs I requested as I went through school and college, such as passing of exams etc. These were the means of spelling out for me the true message, "Yes, God wants you to go ahead with this, He has marked you out for it." Perhaps I was expecting miracles or some sort of Divine revelation specially for me. I could never get into the minds of other students to see how they felt. I often wondered whether they were fully convinced they had a true vocation or were struggling like me. That's very personal, I thought to myself and I'll just have to discuss my thoughts with the spiritual director.

We had a deep, heavy, soul-searching ten day retreat leading up to ordination and even at that late stage, while we had received Deaconate and we were eighteen in number, one more of our year left at this eleventh hour. This put shock vibes through our class and I felt the effects of this deeply. I admired the bravery of this lad who has remained a personal friend of mine ever since, because he had the courage of his convictions. I thought to myself, would I have the courage to do what he did, or am I just going to drift into this life-long commitment on a very unsure and shaky wicket. There was a real tug o' war going on inside me, but I was still consoled by a sufficient peace of mind, with the firm faith that there was a God who was with me and would help me to become, and, go on to do, what He wanted me to do.

Quite a lot of changes had taken place on the home front, with our house now completely renovated and modernized. I was best man at the wedding of another brother who married, and thought to myself, I'll be able to marry the rest of them myself. The little farm held mostly a few grazing cattle by now and most family members were beginning to find their calling in life. The cattle drovers were off the road and lorries had replaced them; it was a similar story with the bog men. Rail and road traffic was increasing rapidly. Amid all this, great preparations were being made in the family home, for the big day of the ordination followed by the first mass. Relatives near and distant were contacted. The ceremony took place for all seventeen of us in the Diocesan College Chapel at Clonliffe, Dublin, May 17th 1964. I understood exactly what I was taking on, but being human, I had apprehensions, anxieties and fears. However, I took on the role with faith and courage, with hope and expectations, determination and ambition. While it was a wonderful and proud day for my parents and family members, they had no idea what was going on in my mind. Nevertheless I felt in so far as I could comprehend it at the time, I was taking on the ministry for my own reasons, and with God's help intended fully to try my best to implement what was expected of me. The first Mass was in Latin, as Vatican 11 had only begun to be introduced. The priest had his back to the people and there was very little English. Several hundred people attended a reception at which I felt I acquitted myself reasonably well in speech and decorum, but the words of the proud old Parish Priest on the occasion still ring out in my ears. "This young man Eamonn has taken on a way of life that has good times and bad times, its ups and downs, its successes and failures, and these could be applied to any walk in life, but if I were to mention the greatest challenge in the priestly life, then that would have to be the loneliness that goes with it."

# CHAPTER FOUR

## APPOINTMENTS PART I

### *Ravenswell Convent and school*
In July 1964 my first appointment was as Chaplain to Ravenswell Convent and adjoining school on the outskirts of a very busy seaside resort called Little Bray, just on the south side of the main town. That particular month would have been peak season and in the sixties Bray could be compared to the Brighton, or Southend of England. July was the month when huge numbers came down from Northern Ireland to avoid the marching season, and likewise large contingents arrived from Scotland. It was a town buzzing with business and had all the usual seaside attractions and amusements, it even had a cable car link to the top of Bray Head. It was not a great beach by any means being rather stony with a steep descent to the water making it quite dangerous. Still it had an attraction for many people at that time as the place to be and of course it was a stepping stone to all the attractive scenery of Co. Wicklow, the Garden of Ireland. Every household tried to make the best of what was on offer with so many tourists around, therefore almost every house became a B&B. Children and many family members lived in back garden shelters, tents and any make-shift shed that was available, to make room for the guests. As I had no accommodation with my appointment, it was up to myself at the time, like many others in my profession, to go and sort out my own arrangements as to where to live. The local curate was at the convent, the morning I arrived for my

first official Mass, and he said "I don't know what they sent you here for, I'm the chaplain here." So this small community of about twelve nuns, with a tiny eight teacher school, now had two chaplains. There were so many priests at the time, the authorities didn't know what to do with us.

Attached to the convent chapel, where daily Mass was said, there was a nice little single unit with a sitting room, bedroom and bathroom. This was unoccupied and I asked the nuns if they would allow me to use it until such time as I found a place of my own. They knew obviously how extremely busy Bray was and how impossible it was to get a bed for love or money in the middle of July. They said, "No, those rooms are for the missioner when he comes to give a retreat." I asked when was he coming. They answered, "Whenever he comes." In other words he was not expected for the foreseeable future and so this unit would lie idle. I was there with one suitcase and a bike on my very first day of my very first appointment, and with very dim prospects of finding a bed anywhere before night-fall. This order of nuns was ironically called "Sisters of Charity." This was extremely poor form on their part, and a very bad start for me. By the way, the local curate was no better, he was there listening and also heard my plight, and made no offer of a bed for a night or two until I found something for myself even though he had a large house which he occupied alone. In fact he had made it quite obvious that he didn't want me there at all in the first place.

Under a compliment I was allowed to leave my case in the sacristy, while I set off down the noisy hectic seaside town. I was dressed in my clerical gear, as we had to at that time and setting out about ten in the morning, I knocked on doors all day, getting the same answer, "Sorry Father, you know the way it is in July, if it was the end of August, you'd be all right. One lady who had a large guest house on the sea front felt sorry for me and told me if I was really stuck at the end of the day, I could use the couch in the lounge when all the residents had gone to bed. I continued my searching and knocking until nearly 9 p.m. with not a hope in sight. So I returned to my only offer and explained I'd be glad to use the couch because at this stage I was desperate and totally exhausted. So having retrieved my suitcase without even an inquiry as to whether I got fixed up or not, I knew at least I'd have somewhere to lay my head for that night. It was always well after midnight when the final guests would retire to bed, then I'd pull out the dual-purpose couch into a bed and as I was up and gone by 6.30am with Mass at 7am I never returned until late that night, trying to find things to do either around the school or parish to keep myself occupied for the day. This beginning was soul destroying and I wondered if it was the same for the other lads in my year. They all had their stories to tell but nothing quite like mine with the cold and indifferent welcome I had received. At weekends I helped with confessions and Sunday Masses and then took an area of the parish to visit families.

The convent provided breakfast only, so I had my other meals in restaurants or hotels. For the first time I was attracted to the game of golf and acquired a secondhand bag and a few clubs. As the door to the sacristy backed on to the third tee of Little Bray nine hole golf course, I got permission from the club to play a few holes in the mornings. I had my clubs stacked away among the vestments and after Mass and breakfast, I'd slide out the back door and off I'd go down the third fairway. I took some lessons in the nearby Woodbrook Club and so in no time I got the bug and golf became a favourite sport.

As the summer season was beginning to ease off, I sought better and more permanent accommodation, and got in with a nice family nearer the centre of the town. The middle-aged parents of this family, bought themselves a car and neither could drive, so I offered to teach them both what I knew about it. The mother was a big stout lady and the father a small bald-headed man, they looked like a Laurel and Hardy couple. It was a brand new car and she being my first pupil picked it up very quickly and actually passed her test first time. He took a little longer, as he was nervous, but he also passed. I was very proud of this achievement and became life long friends of that family. I had a visit home occasionally on a weekend, travelling by two buses, the total journey being about thirty five miles. It was at this time I got my own little car, the very first, a Morris Minor, BRI 83, nicknamed the "Brier" and I got great value out of it. Coming back one night along the canal, there was a bad fog, and young kids were offering to sit on the bonnet and direct people for a little charge. When they heard I was going to Bray they just said, "Go ahead we're not walking back from there." A couple of miles away from the canal, the fog cleared. I got to know a scout group from Arklow and often went on Summer camp with them to help out. This first appointment was for six months only and then I got my second which was as chaplain to an enclosed order of Carmelites in Ranelagh, plus chaplain to St. Ann's Hospital Northbrook Rd, just around the corner, which was a cancer hospital. I was in my new job before Christmas of 1964.

### *Ranelagh*

I became chaplain to an enclosed order of nuns in Ranelagh and for the first time I saw a true spirituality in nuns. They had concern about people's well being, they were interested in my ministry and the fact that I was just beginning on a road that was to change so much in every way that their prayers and support gave me a great feeling of belonging. They had an appreciation of any little kindness offered to them and of course that would encourage one to do so much more for them. I was at the same time, chaplain to the nearby hospital, St. Ann's of Northbrook Rd., where patients were suffering from cancer in all its stages and severity, many had the external form which was very difficult to face every day. I found the enclosed sisters a great support with their prayers both for myself and when I needed them to help with extremely ill and distressed patients. The hospital was also run by nuns, so I was surrounded on all sides by them. I found it interesting how one order differed so much from another.

There were hospital staff meetings on a regular basis at which I was made welcome to discuss the welfare of the patients. The big question arose almost daily regarding whether particular patients should be told about their cancer or not. Doctors, nurses, sisters, and myself would have various opinions to express on the issue, and each case had to be taken separately, delicately, and with all the background circumstances considered. These discussions were always very professional, friendly and discreet. There was never any friction or tension if different opinions were expressed. The welfare of the patients in all cases, young, middle aged or old, both physical and mental, was at all times, the sole and primary aim. We were by no means infallible, and sometimes got it quite wrong, but we did try very carefully and on many occasions were rewarded by fruitful results. It was an interesting psychological fact that those who were told of having cancer would deteriorate much faster than those who were not told, even though the latter in many cases would be much more seriously ill. This proves the theory of mind over matter when it comes to an illness, particularly when it's of the terminal nature. One young patient stands out in my memory, he was a nine year old boy, born with cancer, who never saw his tenth birthday. He was from a small town in Kilkenny called Mullinavat, and was a lovely chatty sort of lad. I asked him how he compared Mullinavat with the capital. He said, "Dublin is only trottin' after Mullinavat." For the first time now I felt I was beginning to do what I set out to do, i.e. to help people in need. There was great scope for that in the hospital. It gave me a sense of being able through the Christian message to give these people some feelings of real dignity in their plight and encourage them to accept their illness and death in a truly Christian manner.

Finding a place to live was again on the agenda and while it was nothing in comparison to Bray, nonetheless, I had to travel a fair distance from my place of work, as Ranelagh and Rathmines were even at that time swamped with university students. So two more senior colleagues who were already sharing digs in a family situation, informed me that there was a bed available in the same house in Sandymount, about twenty minutes away. Since I had my little "Brier," still going well, I took the offer. The other two were chaplains to convents nearby. The lady of the house provided an evening meal which was never good. There was a story told of a workman from the buildings living in the same digs who availed of the evening meal. He loved some mustard and as it was never around, he brought his own in the form of a little tube, resembling toothpaste. After the lady of the house gave him his meal one evening, he proceeded to put a sliver of mustard from the tube on his plate as he usually did, which with its colour and shape looked rather dubious. It happened one evening, totally out of character, the landlady returned to the room for something she'd forgotten and with horror saw this most unusual piece of something on the side of her lodger's plate. Without hesitation she proceeded to wipe it off with the cloth she was carrying saying, "Them bloody hens are everywhere." Our own meals were so bad and greasy at times, we had to burn them in the fire.

Apart from my two official chaplaincy jobs in Ranelagh, I also helped out in Sandymount, Rathmines, and Rathgar, hearing confessions mostly. We got £1 per hour remuneration for hearing confessions in those days. This was always very useful as money was scarce. I had built up some savings in one of these parishes, being owed £30 which I intended to use on my holiday, but despite every possible effort to extract the money from a certain Parish Priest, I never got paid. I was bitterly disappointed and very disillusioned in my early and innocent days that anybody, especially a fellow priest, could be so devious and dishonest. Life at the time was simple and very routine. I retired not later than 10pm as there was an early rising each day, and my only little bit of entertainment was a small battery radio on which I listened to my favourite music at the time, ceili band sounds.

At least in this appointment I had the hospital as basic work and there was always something to be done about the place. I got a small public address system installed on the wards so that patients could follow whatever went on in the oratory and that remained for many years later until they upgraded it to T.V. monitors. But I learned a lot during my eighteen months spent there which in fact prepared me for the next chaplaincy which was to be another and much bigger hospital.

### St. Michael's Hospital, Dun Laoghaire

It was about 11.30am in mid July 1965 as I was putting a few items into a tiny office at St.Michael's Hospital, Dun Laoghaire, having been appointed as the new Chaplain, when shock waves plus thick black smoke covered the whole of the town. Cries of horror and disbelief could be heard as people shouted, "The parish church is on fire." Yes on the very morning of my arrival, the famous and beautiful old Church of St.Michael's was burned to a shell, leaving only the steeple cum belfry standing. This fire was always associated with me coming to the place. Apparently an electrical fault occurred up in the rafters, which had been treated not long prior to this with some protective substance which was highly flammable. As the sacristan was clearing up after the 10am mass, smoke and flames spread as quickly as one could walk from one end of the church to the other. It could not be got at as it was between ceiling and outer roof. The priest had just enough time to remove the Blessed Sacrament before the whole building was engulfed. I abandoned my unloading and joined the many hundreds of people at the scene to watch the tragic destruction. To add to the difficulties, water hydros were scarce, and so there was little water available. The firemen had to try and pump water from the sea which meant there was little or no pressure to enable it to reach the now raging flames. The church was completely destroyed, apart from the spire which remained standing. Very quickly a prefabricated building was erected nearby which served as the parish church for several years while the new and much more modern one was being built. I helped out in this temporary church for the time I was at the hospital.

Finding digs was a factor once again and for nearly a week I was commuting daily from Sandymount. I was very lucky to persuade the elderly lady who had housed my predecessor, to take me in also. She really wished to cease the service as she felt age was catching up on her. She was a most kind and gentle lady and having agreed eventually to take me, she was just like a mother in every way. Her house was about two miles from the hospital which was a very busy general hospital, admitting many serious cases and a lot of accidents. Sick and emergency calls were frequent, day and night. I remember having to get up and rush down five times one night and although I went back to bed each time, I didn't sleep. The old reliable "Brier" was still going strong and clocked up many more miles during this time. Among some of my classmates, there was a regular poker game, which rotated around our venues. I had a very early start each morning, and these sessions often went on to the early hours of the morning. I would arrange with the operator at the hospital to phone me at a certain hour, pretending it was a sick call and therefore assuring me of an early finish. But these smart fellas quickly copped on to this and called my bluff, especially if I was winning at the time of the call.

The hospital was also a training centre for new recruits to the nursing profession. A new private nursing home, run by the same order of nuns, had just opened down at the back and that was my responsibility also. I had a good relationship with the nurses both qualified and trainees. I started some chat sessions of a general nature for groups of the trainee nurses which went very well and built up a good rapport all round, but unfortunately some of the senior staff, whether out of jealousy or sheer spite, claimed I was stirring things up and creating a dichotomy between senior and junior staff. Hardly a day passed but some amusing incident occurred to give a little light-hearted touch to a sometimes difficult scene. The sister in charge of the male medical ward was a great character; rough but likable. She let a roar one day that could be heard all over the hospital, "What nurse put the ice cream in the oven?"

A young trainee nurse was put in charge of a particular patient and was told under no circumstances was she to let him out of bed. One day, he had an urgent call to the bathroom, he needed the commode as the bottle wasn't enough. So to keep to the rule of not letting him out of bed, she placed the commode standing up on the bed and put the patient sitting on it, leaving him elevated way over the surround curtains, so that he had a view all over the ward, but everyone could see him also, it was a very funny sight to behold.

Two little old ladies who were close friends, happened to be in the hospital and coincidentally they were in beds next to one another. Neither of them was at all happy about being in hospital. One of them had returned from surgery and her friend was watching her closely, until she woke up, and of course she asked her the usual question, "Are ya all right?" And then she asked her, "Mary tell me are you gettin' a new dress?" "No, why do you ask?" And she answered, "Because while you were sleepin', they were measuring you for something." They were funny but constantly giving out about something in a light-hearted way. The one back from surgery was asked by the nurse did she want a bed pan. And she answered, "Don't tell me I have to fry me own breakfast as well."

Sunday Mass in the chapel was well attended by a good mix of surgeons, doctors, nurses at all levels and about twenty-five nuns. I tried to present it in such a way that there was a message for all those attending with their various levels and needs. After some weeks I noticed the vestments and the missal I was given to use were very old and tattered and quite disgraceful on any day not to mention Sunday. But laid out in the sacristy nearby were beautiful vestments and a new missal.

I asked the sacristan nun, who was a chubby red-faced, small statured person, if I could use the more presentable set, especially on Sundays with such a mixed and distinguished congregation. "No," she told me, they were for the MONSIGNOR, who came at a later time to say Mass privately at a small side altar, with nobody but the server present. I decided to dig my heels in one Sunday morning and refused to go out to begin Mass unless I was allowed to use the better, more presentable vestments and books. But the little nun, now with a redder face, refused point blank to give in. I told her I was not going out without them. The nuns and people in the chapel were growing impatient, when eventually the Reverend Mother, knowing I was in there waiting, stormed into the sacristy to inquire what the problem was and when I explained my predicament, she told the little chubby one to give me whatever I needed immediately. Well things started flying in all directions, with temper oozing from the now tomato-like face, and she said to me in a most arrogant and loud tone of voice, "Well you are a cheeky little brat." The relationship with this nun and a few more like her at the convent, got worse rather than better for my entire period as chaplain. The tension which existed, even though it was only a small minority who caused it, created in me a rather nervous disposition, and I began for the first time to experience panic attacks. One evening to my great embarrassment I had to leave the altar in the middle of devotions, and go to my office. They sent a doctor to me to ask what was wrong, but I just brushed the whole thing off and did not discuss it with anyone. It took me many years to fight off these attacks which often occurred during a public Mass or ceremony, and if I had buried my pride and sought help, I could have saved myself a lot of pain and suffering. Later in life when I developed a liking for alcohol, I often used these attacks as an excuse to drink more. This in fact only made the situation worse. When finally I succeeded in achieving a contented life without alcohol, then the problem of these panic attacks ceased to bother me.

I admired greatly the nurses who found the training and exams very difficult, because I could identify with them from my own early testing days with books and study. The interesting fact is that more often than not, those who struggled with the books turned out to be better nurses than the more supposedly brilliant. I now had chalked up two years in this ministry and was in for the shock of my life with the most unexpected news of my next appointment.

# CHAPTER FIVE

## LONDON HOTEL CHAPLAINCY

I had just completed my second year as chaplain at St. Michael's Hospital Dun Laoghaire, when, one morning as I sat reading my newspaper in the tiny office which I occupied at the hospital, I got a phone call from a classmate of mine asking me how I liked my change, and I asked, "What change?" as I had heard nothing about it. It upset me somewhat that the news was out before it even got to me, and that was explained by the fact that the lines of communication among the local clergy at the time were such that the news of my change was harboured by them and discussed abroad before it was given to me. But I was to be further shocked and perturbed when I was informed of my destiny.

Without any consultation from superiors or authorities, I was being sent as Hotel Chaplain to the very heart of London, i.e. the West End, to live in Golden Square, adjacent to Piccadilly, Soho and all of that. I had never been to London before and the thought of working and living there for three to five years was both frightening and challenging. A chaplaincy scheme had been set up in the fifties whereby priests from various dioceses in Ireland were sent on loan to look after the spiritual welfare of the many Irish people who were employed in areas of Britain, like, motorways, factories, hotels etc. The scheme was directed by the Columban Fathers.

I had only two weeks in which to extricate myself from digs and hospital and take up residence at 24, Golden Square,

London W1 which backed onto one of the oldest churches in London, Warwick St. Within the few days that followed, I took a flight to London to meet up with my predecessor to try and learn something of the task I was facing. I had never met this man before and while he was of the Dublin Diocese, he was many years senior to me. One of the first questions I asked him was, if he had any inside information as to who might have put forward my name as his successor. He had no idea and in the few days I had, I hoped to be briefed on contacts and places, and to be given some insight into what the job was all about. In fact, he was so busy himself trying to close a chapter in his life of five hectic years as hotel chaplain in the West End and to start a new appointment as curate in a South Co. Dublin parish that in the end, we spent only part of one day discussing the question of my induction. He introduced me to about three hotels and the relevant personnel and that was the sum total of what was supposed to be a week long briefing on my new appointment. This was my introduction to my London Experience and what was to be for me a most daunting and challenging period in my whole career.

### *Journey to London by car*
My next car after the little Morris Minor was a Volkswagen and I had to borrow the £400 from the bank under a huge compliment. It was into this car I packed my few belongings and set out on what I felt was the journey of my life. The crossing from Dun Laoghaire took nearly four hours and then as night was approaching my aim was to get as far as Birmingham and to stay the night with people I had met some years previous when, as a clerical student, I did a ten day stint in that city on what was called the "Peragrinatio" under the direction of the Legion of Mary. I thought at the time I was going to convert not only Birmingham but the whole of England. I was very glad I had made arrangements to stay with these people as the journey took me longer than expected in

the difficult rainy and windy conditions of the night. I was told to stay on the A5 which would take me through Birmingham and eventually on to London.

It was in the early hours of the next morning that I found my friends and with no phones (not to mention mobiles), there was no way of letting them know of my progress or whereabouts, but in fairness to them they were determined to wait up for the entire night if necessary and I was glad of the welcome, food and a night's rest. Being the month of June, the next morning was sunny and warm and so I was on the road again reasonably early, getting back to the A5, as neither the M6 or the upper part of the M1 were built at that time. The remainder of the journey was actually enjoyable, because being on what is now a secondary road, it meant passing through all the towns and villages down the middle of the country.

Having reached this huge city with the then population of 11.5 million, my instructions were to follow the signs to the West End and then to Piccadilly, and there I would find my goal of Warwick St. and Golden Square. I arrived about 4 o'clock in the afternoon and so my new way of life began.

### *Hotel chaplain*

I am not expressing modesty or any form of humility when I say, I was totally unprepared for the task I was about to undertake. As mentioned in the section on school days, I was your average sort of student, just about making it through exams. I was often envious of the honours students when I saw them reach high grades in school and college. Nevertheless I was happy to pass because that was enough for me and it got me through school, seminary and university. With my pass B.A. from U.C.D., Clonliffe Philosophy and Maynooth Theology, and barely two years of pastoral experience, I was being launched into a jungle in the heart of one of the biggest cities in the world. The education I was about to begin could not be found in any school, college or university, nor was there any book written which could explain or prepare anybody for the experiences I was to encounter over the following five years.

Apart from the bare minimum I had achieved in the academic world, I was a very shy, introverted and self-conscious individual. I still had great difficulty in the public speaking area and would be much happier on a one to one basis rather than speaking before a crowd. But as I was now about to be thrown in the deep end, I had to sink or swim, and coming from a family of ten and having been brought up with a good sense of fighting my corner, I decided from day one in London, to give it a go, to offer what I had, just as I had it, and not to try to present a front or a show that would be false and therefore doomed to failure. For reasons that would carry me off on complicated tangents, I've decided not to mention any specific names of the many prominent and excellent people who preceded me on the emigrant team, but just to say that they laid foundations, through extremely hard work, without which, those of us who succeeded them could not have carried on the mission of chaplains to the Irish Emigrants in London and throughout England. It would have been foolhardy of me to try to imitate them or be like them in any way. I wanted to put my own mark on the scene but with one firm intention, that any projects initiated, would be independent of me.

The emigrant chaplains in the London area were on loan to the Westminster Diocese and under the direction and guidance of the Columban Fathers who were at that time based in Ovington Sq. and who later moved to North London. These men had a wealth of missionary experience from many countries throughout the world and therefore were invaluable to us chaplains in guiding us through the pastoral labyrinth of the London scene. When people heard I was a hotel chaplain in London, the first question they asked was "What's that?" Well it does take a little explaining when you consider the traditionally accepted role associated with the priest in Ireland at the time. It was some time before I could answer the question as it took me years to realize myself what was involved.

I was given a warm welcome by the then Rector of the church and Parish Priest of what was I suppose a unique Parish in the heart of London. While being very English and being a highly respected Monsignor in the Diocese of Wesminster, I found him warm, welcoming and most kind and that was a great start for me. I knew straight away that I would like this man who would not make life difficult for me or in anyway hinder the work I was about to begin. Despite his obvious academic and scholarly achievements, he was fun-loving and so simple in his conversation, that he made me and everyone who came to the house most warmly welcomed and totally included in what was happening at the time. Very often he would have well-known film actors and actresses, famous theatrical personalities and such like, invited to lunch at the house and he would always give me ample notice of their coming so that if possible, he would give me the opportunity to meet his special guest. This happened quite regularly but unfortunately the Monsignor's stay at Warwick St. Church was only to be for the first two years of my stay. Soon he moved to a higher status as the Dean of Westminster Cathedral.

My first and urgent task was to try and find my way around the streets of this part of the city and for at least the first week or more I never used the car once. I had it parked in a multi-storey car park costing much more than I could afford. I was afraid I would get completely lost in the labyrinth of one-way streets. So having made contact with a fellow-diocesan who had arrived shortly before me to start work as a curate in the densely Irish populated parish of Euston, he was in the same boat as myself (lost), we both walked the streets for days and nights trying to figure out the directions, especially the one-way system. Each time we got lost of course, but that was good because we learned a lot in trying to find our way back to base. We were to work closely together over the next three or four years and very often organized outings or functions bringing together our two communities of Irish people.

The principal idea behind my chaplaincy to the hotels and many others who were working either on building sites, motorways or in factories or parishes, was to keep contact with Irish people. The chaplain aimed to be with them as much as possible in all their walks of life and in many cases that presented him with a variety of problems, a lot of which would never be found in Dublin or in any part of Ireland. As the year was 1967, the post-war fifties and sixties glut of emigrants had still left a lot to be desired, and many difficult roads to travel for a great number of young Irish boys and girls. So, while the chaplain's main interest was the spiritual welfare of his flock, he was also very much like a social worker, because the newly-arrived emigrant would often turn to the established priest or chaplain seeking accommodation, work, and immediate assistance in their new life in the big city. The bureau in Dublin which was only growing at the time, would try and give those intending emigrants who asked for guidance, a contact name and number, depending on where they arrived and what sort of work they sought.

### *Warwick Street Church*

If one were to do justice to this beautiful little church, the entire book could be devoted to it. But perhaps a few facts and dates about it might encourage people to visit it while in London. The church was originally built in 1790 as the Bavarian Embassy Chapel, and the embassy itself backed onto Golden Square. As it was developed over the years into the church it is today, it was regularly visited by Royalty from England, Bavaria and other parts of the world. They in turn would have left a particular mark of remembrance, and so a statue or altar might be added. There are many features of interest including the ceiling, the wooden pews in the gallery, baptismal font, and the iron gallery railings. Over the centre door there is a plaque in perspex, set in a gilded frame and bearing the royal arms of Bavaria. Also noteworthy are the oval stations of the cross with a delicate "Wedgewood" appearance; a statue of St. Anthony of Padua; a fine marble altar dedicated to the patron of the church, St. Gregory the Great, who for the first half century of this church's life, was the only patron. Over the altar is a carved and painted statue of St. Gregory. High up on the east wall over the sacristy door there is a large plaque of the Assumption of the Blessed Virgin Mary.

One of the most interesting features of Our Lady's altar is the presence of many silver hearts around the shrine and this amazes people. In 1877 the rector of that period obtained a Papal Decree from Pius 1X dated May 15$^{th}$ of the same year officially approving the shrine and bestowing blessings and indulgences on all those who devoutly visit it. The framed decree now hangs beneath the statue of Our Lady. The terms of the decree and the numerous indulgences granted to those who visit and pray at the shrine strongly suggest that a lively cult of the Blessed Virgin had existed there for some time.

The Monsignor of the time initiated and encouraged the custom of hanging up votive hearts or medals, given in thanksgiving for favours received. Large numbers of these objects were donated, until the walls of the chapel became covered with them. He and his successors have been criticised for allowing such things to be put up in the church, but in doing so he was only following a custom widespread on the continent. In the years that followed the number of medals and silver hearts was reduced and just a token few around the Shrine of Our Lady remain today.

### *Launching into the unknown*
Waking up to the first day of my work as Hotel Chaplain was nothing short of negotiating a jungle of pitfalls. Where in God's name was I to start? How do I go about the ministry when I enter a hotel? I first equipped myself with an A-Z of London and decided to try and find at least one or two of the

hotels on my list, and then perhaps one thing would lead to another, a new name or contact. Thus it all began when I arrived at the Mayfair Hotel looking for the head housekeeper.

I decided from day one, especially when trying to introduce myself to people for the first time, to wear my clerical garb. In that way at least they knew more or less what I was and I'd only have to explain what denomination. It took me a while to become accustomed to many people calling me "Vicar", or "Reverend." After a phone call from the desk I was told to make my way to the fifth floor and ask the attendant to show me to the head house-keeper's office. This lady, although very English, was also very Catholic and she was completely on my side. She not only knew my predecessor very well, but also knew and spoke very highly of all the previous chaplains who had pioneered this work from its infancy to that time. She was of Irish descent but was born and reared in London and had an accent you could cut with an knife. Then she informed me that she was more than just the head house-keeper, she was the "executive" head house-keeper.

My first impressions of her were not good, in fact, "very off-putting" would be more accurate, but before I left her office that day I realized that she was going to be a key person in support and help to me, i.e., giving me names and contacts in all the big fancy hotels of the West End. Like any other fraternity, the hotel personnel, knew one another and had a mutual and widespread understanding among themselves. While very much a practising Catholic, she also had a good relationship with the Irish, especially those working in her own hotel. At the same time she held a very responsible position and therefore was very business-like in her approach to everything. Her manner would give the impression of being very hard and almost ruthless in dealing with people. That was the nature of her role, but behind it all, as I was to realize in the weeks and months that followed, she was a kind and caring person who became in fact a very good friend of mine and I was privileged to be invited to her home for meals and socials and then to be an adviser in her personal life and relationships. In her late forties, I was to see her marry her partner during my time in London. To this day she keeps in contact by Christmas cards, and she visits whenever she's in Ireland. I concluded my first hotel visit eventually, feeling I was treated generously both in time given and information obtained and I felt that I had in fact done a good day's work and had enough to chew on for the rest of that day and perhaps it might take me that long anyway to find my way home to base.

My accommodation at Golden Sq., was on the third floor of a five storey building and consisted of one average size room which was, sitting room cum office, and general purpose with a small bedroom adjoining. Bathroom and toilet facilities were off the landing. The rooms were simply furnished with the basic requirements and in a short time I added my own personal effects to try and make it as homely and welcoming as I could. It was as they say "an all-found situation." I was entitled to full board and lodging as I so wished. As for parish responsibilities, I was expected, on certain designated days, to say the lunch-time Mass and hear confessions and at weekends to be available for confessions and say at least two, sometimes more, Sunday masses. After that, my time was my own, and, I was not expected to be on call for any of the other parish duties. I was free to come and go as I wished in carrying out my duties, as chaplain to the Irish in the West End hotels. My official salary was £8 per month which rose to £9 after three years. If it had not been for family and Dublin Diocesan support I could not have survived.

One of the many outstanding memories I have, happened one weekday when I was hearing confessions, followed by the lunch time Mass. I was preparing and vesting for Mass, when an American tourist arrived into the sacristy laden down with cameras and bags and he was very colourfully dressed. He asked if I would offer a Mass for all his deceased relatives who were Irish and he made it abundantly clear that one mass for the entire list was his wish. He was on his way to Ireland and would have loved a long chat, but he realized that I had a tight schedule with lunch time people in the Church waiting for mass. I put the envelope with the list of names and stipend into my pocket and proceeded to celebrate the lunch time Mass. It so happened that I had arrangements to meet some friends that evening and share a meal on a "go dutch" basis and I literally did not have a shilling in my pocket. I was sick and embarrassed at the thought of having to ask for a loan but I had no choice. It was mid-afternoon when I became conscious of the envelope in my pocket from the American tourist and I opened it to have a look at the list of names. I expected maybe a couple of dollars stipend, but no, to my great surprise and absolute delight, there was a £50 pound sterling note. That was a lot of money in 1967 and when I thought of my plans for my night out later and being saved the embarrassment of looking for a loan, and being entitled to keep this stipend, I was delighted. I felt the Lord had literally sent me manna from Heaven. I had a great night out and I offered a very special Mass for the donor's intentions.

## *Special dispensation*

Due to the fact that hotel workers have unusual working hours, a special dispensation was given to have a mass at 4 o'clock in the afternoon on Sundays to try and accommodate them. This was granted long before the vigil mass or Sunday evening mass. It had been up and running for a number of years prior to my arrival and by then the novelty had to some extent worn off, but it was still very popular and was in addition attended by many people outside of the hotel fraternity. The practice of the Sunday 4 o'clock mass was still there up to recent years and was celebrated by the hotel chaplain. After this Mass one Sunday two elderly English ladies came to me to say how much they enjoyed it, especially the homily, and of course feeling very elated by the comments I wished to prolong the compliments by asking what message they had received from the homily and they replied: "Oh, we don't know what it was about, but it was very good." That brought me back to earth very quickly!

## Pilgrimages and outings

In the course of each year, several groups would travel to Lourdes for either a few days or even just an all night vigil. On one of these three day pilgrimages, I had persuaded a house keeper, an English Church of England lady, who thought the Rosary beads was a necklace, to come with us. Although she was anti-Catholic and anti-Irish, she thought the little holiday would do her good and perhaps it might help her asthma. She agreed to join the queue and go to the baths, provided I waited for her nearby. When she eventually emerged she joined me at the edge of the adjoining River Gave, and there she got a serious asthma attack in front of me. It was so bad that the ambulance was called and she ended up in hospital for that night. In the months that followed I had to endure many smart comments on that event. Sometimes we joined with other areas of London and went on a couple of pilgrimages to Rome. These were great fun but because of the extra expense involved, it meant we had a rather select group who could afford it.

There were many outings to places like Brighton, the Isle of Wight and on one occasion we did an over-land trip to Paris, all for £7 a head return, in the year 1969. One I won't forget was a trip to the Southend illuminations. I had nearly a hundred people booked on two coaches and as we loaded the passengers on at Golden Sq., one of the drivers quietly said to me, "Do you realize Sir the illuminations at Southend finished last weekend for the season?" What could I do at this stage but run with it and during the pub break, I told them there would be no lights at the end of our journey. We made the break a little longer than scheduled and by the time we got back on the road they didn't mind if there was no Southend, not to mention lights!

All of these pilgrimages and outings were very valuable occasions for getting to know people and many relationships developed which would not happen in the work place. From the bonding that emerged, the need for some sort of meeting place became necessary, as a drop-in-centre or club to socialize locally and safely, and from that the Grotto Club was born. The cellar area underneath the house and Church of Golden Sq. and Warwick St. was made available to us. So we developed it into a nice club atmosphere with bar licence and catering facilities included. I'm so happy to say that the club is still there today.

### *Would you believe?*
Apart from breakfast and the odd lunch, I was never in the house much for meals. On occasions at breakfast I played the role of referee between two of the staff at the time. These were priests attached to the presbytery. One was very English and the other very Irish. It was approaching the early seventies when things were beginning to heat up in the North of Ireland, and the former in question would be buried behind his "Times," saying very loudly, "These bloody Irish are killing all our British soldiers," and while lowering his "Irish Press," the latter would say, "What are ya talkin' about, it's a just war isn't it?" That would be the opening of an encounter that would need more than a referee.

I was all set to go home for Christmas one year, when the foot and mouth disease became a problem on both sides of the water. All travel except the absolute essential was disallowed. So while in the Aer Lingus office in Regent St. cancelling my ticket, I was interviewed by B.B.C. television news as one of the many passengers who was so disappointed not to be travelling home for Christmas.

Making my way back to base one day for the lunch-time 1 o'clock Mass I noticed not far down the street I was walking, two "ladies of the night" were out looking for business very early. I was all dressed in my full clericals and as I approached, they were conniving and giggling, preparing to have a comical encounter with me. They both actually blocked my pathway and said, "Would you like a nice time, Vicar?" Off the top of my head I just said, "I'm in a hurry now, but I'll see ye all later," just to run with their fun. When I looked back at them, they were simply doubled up on the footpath laughing. Don't you start guessing now, I did not go back later. Soho at that time was full of strip clubs and many of the girls working there as strippers, would regard that as any ordinary job while they were at the same time in a married relationship and might even be church-going Christians.

## *Challenges*

On arriving quietly at the presbytery at 2am one morning after a visit to an Irish dance hall, I got the distinct smell of cigarette smoke. It was the "fresh" and not the "stale" sort of smell, as in the aftermath of a smoking crowd in a house. I sensed the presence of someone nearby at that moment who must have been smoking. I would not be satisfied until I saw for myself what was going on. I decided to investigate and proceed through the passage that led to the church. As I entered the small area immediately outside the sacristy door, there, sitting on a bench smoking a cigarette was this stranger, calm, cool, relaxed and in no hurry to evade or hide from my approach. I was the first to speak. "Are you looking for someone?". "No, not really," he said, "I just broke into your place and I did not know it was a church, and if I did know, I would not have done this." "Where did you gain entry" I asked. "Through the cellar window, come and I'll show you," he said. "Don't be afraid, I'm not going to assault or attack you," he re-assured me.

We went to the cellar together and right enough he showed me the broken window where he had gained entry. He then asked me to come back up to the church to show me that he had left a note on one of the shrines apologizing for what he had done. He said he had stolen nothing, and that he would come back some day to pay for the damage to the window. Then he looked at me as if he was saying, well what are you going to do with me now, I was asking myself the very same question.

The Parish Priest at the time was a fussy old guy and if he became aware of what was going on in his presbytery and his church at this hour of the morning, the whole of the West End would have been awoken. I really don't know what made me decide to do what I did. I asked the intruder if he would walk with me to the local police station, which was Saville Row, about six or seven minute's walk. He agreed and off we went. I quizzed him as we walked as to why he had broken in and what he was looking for. He explained that he had got a real shock when he realized it was a church and that was why he made no attempt to hide when I entered. As we crossed Regent St. I was convinced he would just make a run for it (in fact that was my secret plan) and I was not going to give chase, but would just proceed and report the burglary at the police station. He did not even attempt to run and we entered the station together at almost 3am I told the officer on duty that this man had just broken into our church at Warwick St. "Well, now sir, that's an unusual role for you to be bringing in the burglar, we usually do that job," he said. "I'm very tired right now, could I call back in the morning and give a full report on all this," I said. He agreed and as I left I really felt sorry for my pitiful "prisoner" because he looked at me as if to say, why did you have to bring me down here.

Next morning I was told that this young man was a native of the West Country and that he had a few previous but minor convictions. I asked if I could see him and my request was granted. I reassured him that because of his complete co-operation in all of this affair, he would get a very fair hearing and I further promised to leave a letter that very morning in the station, asking that my report be read out in court. He got a suspended sentence of three months and was back to the house looking for me about ten days later wondering if I would get him that job I mentioned. I got him fixed up as a kitchen porter with accommodation included. He stayed about five weeks, then disappeared off the scene, and I never heard of or saw him afterwards.

In the hostel attached to this same hotel which was the living quarters for the staff there was a waitress I got to know among the staff. She was an English girl and lived with the other girls, socialized with them and in fact had an Irish boy friend. "Julie" was her name, and I often remarked to myself how strong she was as she served at table in the restaurant, carrying large trays full of dinner meals, held up with one hand. As girls often share secrets, one confided in "Julie" that she was pregnant, and so "Julie" reciprocated by sharing her own secret, which was that "she" was a boy and not a girl. Her so-called friend could not stomach this but reported it to the house keeper. All hell broke loose that afternoon as "Julie" was taken away by police. This turned out to be a twelve year old boy from the midlands of England, an only child, who really wished to be a girl from early age. His mother was separated from the time of his infancy and so he had never known what it meant to have a father. The talk among the girls in the hostel afterwards was interesting when I heard them say things like, "Imagine that Julie thing living here with us exchanging clothes, doing the ironing, and what about the poor eejit of a boy friend!" There were many stories and cases where the chaplain was called in and made feel part of the situation.

### *Risks*

There are many things which could be said and done in the sixties and seventies that today would be unacceptable and counter-productive. When I think back on some of them I am somewhat amazed myself. Getting people fixed up in jobs and accommodation meant regular trips to the airport to pick up new arrivals and so the M4 was very familiar. Returning to the city one afternoon with a really full load of passengers and luggage hanging from the back tied with a piece of rope, I had a near escape when a little "yuppie" broke the lights, resulting in me having to swerve sharply and I ended up on the footpath, almost crashed through a shop window, and for my huge load it was much more than just a sudden drop in cabin pressure. I said nothing but got back on the road immediately and set off pursuing the offender. It was a while before my passengers realized I was travelling in the wrong direction, but I said, "Hold on I've got to do this." There was a hold up at the traffic lights ahead and not many cars on, I could see the guy I was after, I got out of my car and quickly walked to his. I knocked on his window and said, "You nearly caused an accident back there by breaking the lights" and he said "What lights?" With that I opened his door, and with my fingers tightly down his shirt collar, I had him out across the bonnet of his car in seconds and I said "Now, I'll tell you what lights I'm talking about." "I'm sorry, I'm sorry, I'm sorry, I was distracted and did not realize what I had done," he said. "That's all I wish to hear, but don't get smart and don't forget this lesson today." That to me was far better than reporting it to a police station and never hearing about it again. He learned a lesson and I was satisfied. Meanwhile the passengers in my car were gob-smacked, not to mention the many howling motorists, by now a long line, held up because of me.

On another occasion, I had arrangements made to leave a girl to the airport who was returning home to Ireland permanently, and when I arrived at her flat to pick her up, I found her sitting on the landing, crying and distressed. "What's wrong?" I asked. "The door slammed behind me" she said, "and everything, key, luggage, tickets, the lot, are inside. There's no one else in the house. "What am I going to do?" she asked pitifully. Realizing that time was tight to make it to the airport for the flight, something had to be done immediately, otherwise, she could forget it until the next day. As the door to her flat had only one light yale lock holding it, with a nice sharp karate kick I had it opened, and we were on our way. I returned some days later to the landlady and explained.

I once again took a major risk one night at the roundabout near Piccadilly Circus, when a large four by four jeep nearly ran me off the road by taking my right-of-way, I pursued at speed and caught him on the wide Pall Mall thoroughfare. I did an American-style pull across the front of the vehicle forcing him to pull in and stop near the curb. I jumped out and went straight to the driver to complain and only then did I realize, there were four big men in this jeep. At this stage I couldn't retract and continued with my protest. To my surprise and relief, all four apologized for their mistake and the fright and danger they had caused me. I was of course totally happy with this and we went our separate ways satisfied and while driving my short journey home slowly and thoughtfully, I reflected on what could have happened. If those guys really wished they could have hit me a few thumps, taken my car and left me for dead.

### Social worker

Very often I felt more like a social worker than a chaplain or a priest. I had a good understanding with many of the hotel directors and managers, where they helped me and I helped them. They had a constant need for staff at all levels and I invariably had people seeking work and accommodation. This had its successes and failures, its surprises and disappointments, but over all, it levelled fairly evenly on both sides. Dealing with the problems of single mothers and their babies was difficult and time-consuming. Again this had its share of successes and failures and a lot of disappointments. I hardly ever recommended a relationship between a coloured foreign national and an Irish girl. This was not racist, but simply that the background and culture in both cases were so far removed, that it hardly ever worked out. If marriage was suggested, and they insisted, I had no problem in recommending a registry office, at least it would only be a civil marriage and so there would be a way out. In 99% of the cases

I met, these girls would return with a very similar story, that their partner had left and they were pregnant.

In 1968 the abortion act was passed in England and that changed the whole area of care for mothers and babies dramatically. I was abhorred and devastated by what I saw and heard. I spent a lot of time in hospitals trying to persuade girls not to have an abortion and I would follow them right down to the theatre making last minute appeals. Babies were thrown out in bins like dead dogs or garbage; to some mothers it meant no more than having a tooth out. An innocent and very nice girl I knew well, was booked for an abortion and I called to her flat the night before, determined I would not give up on this one. Having spent hours talking and assuring her of my total and absolute assistance in my alternative plan, it all went in one ear and out the other. I was annoyed and angry and in her nightie, dressing gown and slippers, I literally dragged her by her long hair down the stairs for loading into my car. With all the commotion the landlord appeared and protested out loud, "What's going on here?" "Mind your own business," I said, and continued with the girl. I took her straight away to a mature and experienced Irish lady, who I knew would take her in and help. Although it was near midnight, she did not complain, when I rang the bell. She was simply great. She took the girl in and stayed out of work the next day to supervise her in case she did a runner. Through sheer grit and determination, this baby which the mother never even wished to see, was born and adopted.

*Memorable places, faces and cases*
There are some memories that will be uppermost in my mind for life. These experiences would never be found anywhere in Ireland at that time. One day, while visiting the upper floors of a hotel where I had complete freedom, and had become a familiar figure around the place, I was accustomed to finding out what room a certain girl might be working in, and this was either by the presence of the trolley outside the door or a towel

hanging on the handle of the door. As I was in the process of organizing an outing to some place I was looking for a certain shy little girl from the West of Ireland. I thought she might like to join us and so I proceeded to the proper floor where I was told she was working and was quickly able to find her whereabouts. When I entered the room, what a shock I got, I'll never forget the scene. From the open doors of the wardrobe two legs were protruding, there was blood all over the floor, and the head and shoulders of a baby appeared from the body of this young girl who was extremely distressed, crying and in great pain. I first grabbed some sheets from the bed and tried to fix them around the area where the baby was by now quickly arriving and I said to her, "Don't worry, you'll be alright, help is on the way." I had my hand under the head and back of a now fully born baby boy. Was I "swettin"? Not knowing how to and with nothing to cut the cord, I held the baby in one hand and with the other managed to reach the telephone and asked the house keeper to come immediately, I told her that this was an emergency. Within minutes the room was flooded with people of all sorts, quickly followed by ambulance personnel who then took over. Mother and baby were soon on their way to a nearby maternity hospital. I think I can lay claim to having delivered my first baby.

Coincidentally, I had another baby experience. One night I got a phone call from my colleague in Euston who had contact with a large number of Irish living in a hostel attached to the station, to say that he was on his way to the hostel having answered a call from the house-keeper there for help in a case something similar to the one I've just described. He thought that having had the experience I might be of some help to him. We met and proceeded to the scene. At least this time I was prepared for something unusual. On a wide landing of the fourth floor of the hostel was a pale-faced frightened girl wrapped in a blanket. Nearby was the house-keeper on her knees with a newly born baby in her lap which was wrapped in a white sheet and she was gently wiping it with water she was taking from a nearby bucket on the floor. Both of us first reassured the young mother who had just given birth. We then knelt down beside the baby and the nursing house keeper. For a few moments no one said a word. Then she spoke up and said "Are either of you gentlemen going to baptize the child?" We both said "Yes" together. Then we asked, "Is it a boy or a girl?" "It's a boy," she said.

So my colleague (Seamus) scooped some water from the bucket and with his dripping cupped hand asked me, "What will I call him?" "Seamus," I answered. "I will not," he said. "I'll call him, Eamonn." "You will not," I answered. With that the old lady house-keeper said, "Call him, Sean." That was the name given to this lovely little baby who then was whisked away with his mother by ambulance to hospital. We laughed on the way home about how the baby got his name.

One never knew what a phone call might entail. A very dedicated mature Irishman who was head of the Pioneer Total Abstinence Association in London called me at 2.30am to say he was in Leicester Sq. Tube Station and that a man had just jumped under the train as it sped into the stop. He had been broken to pieces, and the ambulance had taken away what they could recover. There was no need for me to go to that scene as there was nothing I could do for the poor man.

At a more reasonable hour of 10pm a hotel manager called to know if I would come over immediately as there was a serious disturbance in the kitchen. A Scotsman and a Nigerian (both senior chefs) were attacking one another with large knives. When I arrived, it had calmed down somewhat, and the two people involved (whom I knew) were already back at their work. I was not only allowed in but was welcomed straight into the kitchen to have a word with them while they got on with their work. It was interesting in both those cases that the Catholic Chaplain to the hotels was officially called to the scene. It would be so different today.

There was a lot of night rambling to be done in visiting the pubs, clubs and dance halls. It was tough late night work, but it was at some of these venues that I first began to do the odd gig and although I was very raw at the game, it was a beginning at what was in later years to be the foundation for my participation in the "All Priests Show." A well seasoned manager of a North London dance hall, welcomed me one night and explained to me in his English style Kerry accent what it was all about as we looked around the packed dance floor, which by the way, had no bar facilities, only teas and soft drinks. Being the good Irish host, especially to the priest, this manager had a cup of tea brought over to me, saying "Get that into ya Father, that'll warm ya up on a cauld nite like this." Between many distractions, the cup of tea was left sitting for quite a while, so much so that he reminded me of it when he stuck his mouth into my ear and said, "Don't forget yer cuppa, Father." Knowing that it would be quite cold by this time, I took a big gulp and nearly choked when I tried to swallow it. It was mostly whiskey, and I was not a drinker at that time.

Parking the car was a continuous problem day or night. I had come to an arrangement with the management of N.C.P. (National Car Parks) that I could leave my car over-night at the nearby multi-storey which had recently been opened. Returning from a late-night visit to a dance hall in Kilburn, I parked my car in my usual niche on the second floor and said good night to the attendant who was an Irish lad I knew well. My walk to Golden Sq. at a reasonable pace was about ten minutes and it was a zig-zag through the back streets of Soho. It was about 2.30am and I noticed foot steps behind me, matching mine and taking every left or right turn I took myself. Becoming more conscious of being followed, I changed my usual route and that made no difference to the person following me. In fact the foot steps behind me were quickening and drawing very much closer to me. I always carried a "knuckle duster" with me, especially at night, which had been given to me by a member of the Flying Squad from Scotland Yard, all of whom I had got to know very well. He told me that some night on this dangerous late night walk (which he knew I travelled quite often) I might need such a defensive weapon. I clearly remembered his words to me, "You'll get one chance only, never a second." Luckily I had time to think of all this and not at any stage did I glance back at the person closing in on me from the rear, who may have thought I was unaware of possible danger. By now I had managed to get my defensive weapon inside my glove and ready for action. As they would say in Dublin "I was swettin' bricks." My pursuer came right along side me and spoke, "What time is it sir?" in a soft-spoken English accent. All in one action as I turned, I pulled my right hand from my pocket tightly holding the "knuckle duster" and let fly with all my strength at his nose. He fell to the ground like a ton of bricks and on completing the full turn, I ran for all I was worth and did not stop until I was at No. 24 Golden Sq. I got inside, closed the door leaning up against it full body and sighed a big relief. I was half expecting blue lights and knocking on the door before long. Nothing happened and after a sleepless few hours I made an early call to my friend at the Flying Squad department and explained everything that happened, expecting that I might be charged with assault or whatever; instead he congratulated me in doing exactly as he had instructed me. He remarked that nobody follows a person at that hour in the morning through the streets of Soho, merely to ask the time. It was either him or me and if I had not acted like I did, I would have been the one left lying on the street. It took me days to recover from the experience. That's one face I never saw.

I was finished a hotel visit one afternoon and as I was close to the back, I decided to exit that way as it left me in familiar surroundings. As at the front of the house there was also a rear door porter, and I knew this fellow to be peculiar to say the least, but what I didn't know was that he had a huge grudge against clergy of any denomination. I was not therefore prepared for any sort of dialogue as I left but would respond politely if he uttered any words good or bad. He was standing half blocking the open doorway with one foot almost on the footpath, which meant I had to more or less squeeze past him and as I did I could see he was making a good old swing at me without saying a word. If he had connected I would have been flattened, but I saw the action in time to duck and evade the attempted knock-out. I walked on calmly but he did not pursue. That gave me something to think about as I walked home. I decided not to report the incident to anyone which would almost certainly have cost him his job and possibly leak out as a damaging distorted report and therefore jeopardize my standing in the hotel.

## *London prisons*

About mid-way through my London stint, the Catholic Chaplain to the prisons of Wormwood Scrubbs, Brixton and Holloway got a serious nervous breakdown and subsequently left the ministry. The directors of the Emigrant Chaplaincy, the Columban Fathers, were asked if they could loan a priest for about six months until a new permanent chaplain was found for the prisons. I was asked, if I would do it and if so I would be relieved from the hotel work. I accepted and I'm glad I did, because it was a most memorable experience. Quite frankly I didn't like it and would not take it on a permanent basis. My task basically was to interview all new comers who declared themselves as Catholic. In this way I met quite a large number of Irish men and women in this strange world and everyone of course would swear on their mother's grave to be innocent.

Involvement in the prisons also meant many visits to the court rooms, either speaking on behalf of, or explaining an after-care programme for the accused or maybe just being there to give moral support to someone who asked. One such Irish lad I'll always remember, let's call him "Mikey." He had curly red hair, both eyes badly cast and a loud flat Southern Irish accent. He might have been taken in on suspicion by the mere sight and sound of him. He asked me to be in court for his case which was petty theft, but he had a suspended six months sentence hanging over him and therefore was very likely to go down for the six months. I said I'd be there and would speak on his behalf because he was really an unfortunate and harmless sort of a chap. That's not what the judge wished to hear, but rather he wanted to know who was going to care for him and supervise his future. I could have done all that, but it so happened I was late getting to the courtroom and I arrived in, just after the judge had passed the six months sentence on "Mikey." All I heard the poor devil shout up at the judge was, "Ya big baldy bollocks". "Remove the prisoner", were the only words from the judge.

The prison experience gave me a sense of the British justice system and court room procedure and what it was like inside these places meeting and dealing with people of all sorts. Walking across the courtyard of the women's prison in Holloway one evening, an inmate shouted from the top window, "Would ya like to make love Father, I'm on the second floor?" The lady prison officer with me just told me to carry on and not even to look up. On returning to Ireland I had something to offer and compare with the prisons at home.

## *My stay in hospital*

I had developed a duodenal ulcer from my school days due to long fasting from food and it caught up on me around 1970 in the middle of Holy Week that year and I was taken to a North London hospital for an emergency operation and this whole experience was the cure for my smoking. I was a sixty-a-day man, especially in the prison work, and the surgeon said to me the night before the surgery, "If I don't operate you'll die and if you don't quit the smoking, I won't operate." "I've no choice then, have I ?" "Precisely," was his answer and I've never smoked cigarettes since.

On waking after the surgery, I noticed a jar of caviar beside my bed and when I asked where it came from the nurse told me that, a lady saw me being wheeled from the theatre and said to the attendant, that man looks very bad, give him that when he wakes up. I waited until after the operation to phone home and as I spoke to my parents from the hospital bed they sensed I did not sound the best, and only then I explained. Within a couple of days, two of my brothers made the journey to see me. At first they could not believe it was me, I looked so bad. I was conscious of their presence and many other visitors also. A nun came in and threw my brothers out and everybody else, saying, "No visitors allowed." I don't know where I got the strength from, but I managed to get out of the bed, dragging a drip on wheels and as I caught on the nun down the corridor said, "Sister, don't ever treat my brothers or visitors like that again." Then I fainted, out cold, flat on the floor. I woke up later back in my room with all in order. Ever since that, for the five weeks I was there, the same little nun would pop her head in and say, "Would your visitors like a cup of tea?" I was taken back to Ireland in a wheelchair and told to take six months break. I was back at work in the London hotels after six weeks and went on to complete another two years, bringing my full term on the mission to five.

During my five weeks in hospital, among the many visitors who came to see me, I was surprised one day to see my friend from the Scotland Yard Flying Squad. At the time I was feeling rather sorry for myself trying to recover from major surgery, and his visit was a very significant and uplifting one. During his chat he asked as most people in similar circumstances do, "Is there anything I can do for you?" And like a child, taking advantage of the offer from such an influential person, I told him there was one thing he could do for me which I would really enjoy. And when I told him what it was, he laughed. My request was to be brought in a police car at peak hour right through Piccadilly with sirens, blue flashing lights, plenty of noise and clearance made for a speedy passage. "When you're fully recovered, just give me a call," he said. I don't forget things like that and he kept his promise. The thrill I experienced took me back to childhood and the memory stayed with me ever since.

Being the one who ordained me in 1964 and Archbishop of Dublin at the time, I had a lot of personal contact with John Charles McQuaid during my time on the Emigrant Chaplaincy. He would write to me regularly and include some money which he knew I needed badly. He had personal contact with many unfortunate down-and-outs in Dublin at that time and those who decided to try their luck in London and who went to him prior to their journey, would arrive at my door with a letter from himself including some money, and briefly saying "Look after this lad Father, he's a personal friend of mine." They were all personal friends of his. On my visits to Dublin I would be expected to call to Archbishop's House and give him a full personal report on everything especially his own "charges". I found him to be a kind warm man who had such an interest in people's welfare and in a very special way his own priests.

### *First major career crisis*
After some great but tough years in London and many enjoyable periods of parties and friendships, on my return in 1972, I felt very much attracted to a girl who had been doing a lot of secretarial work for me. I never knew what it meant to be emotionally involved with the opposite sex, or what it meant to really feel that someone loved me and maybe I loved in return.

Having received a lovely appointment near home, which was intended as a sort of a reward for all I'd done, but also to be near my parents and family for my next stage, I found myself making regular trips to London to be with this girl. I could see no way out of it but to consider leaving the ministry and commit the rest of my life to her. I spoke to many of my colleagues, who tried to persuade me not to go down that road. They thought it was not in anyway a proper or even a rational decision for me to make. It was all to no avail, I was completely besotted. The relationship was not at this time and never had been physical or sexual but, an inter-personal relationship that was taking over my complete life and future. My next step was to contact our local G.P. and family doctor whom I'd asked to keep confidence until I was ready and then he and I together would inform my parents first and then the family. But he went ahead and spilled everything long before I was ready to make this all-important move. There was high jinks at home, especially with my mother. My Father however, took me aside quietly, to one of the bed rooms, and spoke to me in a very calm and fatherly manner, the likes of which I could never remember him doing in my entire life to date. This had a lasting and memorable impression on me and this intervention was to change my whole thinking and intended decision. It was not easy. It all took time. There was a lot of pain, anger and hurt, on all sides. But like all of these happenings in life, trust in the Lord, Faith, patience and then time itself, are the best ways of healing and getting on with it, which I did. I became a better person and priest as a result of this experience and thanks to God, family and friends, I went on to do my next ten years in what I felt was fruitful ministry.

### *Changed person*
I had come out of myself and changed so much, I hardly recognized myself. What an education all of this had been. Apart from my slight English accent which only other people noticed, I now had no fear or inhibitions with public speaking, singing a song, telling a funny story, presenting an enjoyable, uplifting and helpful liturgy at mass on Sundays. I had learned to speak clearly, audibly and intelligibly, to be punctual, properly dressed and groomed. A difficult thing for Irish people to practice in their own homeland, is to try to forgive and forget a difference with another person immediately or at least the very next day and although I hadn't perfected this one, by any means, at least I had learned to see the value of it and how important it was to work hard at it, in relations with people. I have to admire English people I had met for this particular quality.

From being a shy, withdrawn and inexperienced person, I had become quite the opposite and all for the correct reasons. There was no school, college, university or books that could have supplied what I now had. They call this the university of life and that's what I'd been through. I have been since ever so grateful for the London experience which was now to set the pattern for the subsequent years.

# CHAPTER SIX

## HOBBIES AND PASTIMES

It was 1972 when I came to Rathcoole from London, and only from then on did I have any opportunity to turn my attention to some sort of systematic form of hobby, pastime or relaxation. The things that interested me were walking, gardening, golf, shooting, house furnishings with a slant on antiques, musical instruments, or just listening to music. The outdoor activities had, keeping fit, in mind because they involved walking or fairly strenuous application. These helped keep me in reasonably good shape and also controlled the weight.

I don't have a great interest in sport but like music, I dabbled in most of what was on offer during school and college years. During my secondary school years, I was honoured to be selected to play on the hurling team to represent the school. Myself and a fellow Kildare lad were told to make our way out to Belfield to play our first match. The two of us set off on the bus to meet up with the other players and supporters at the grounds and not having any idea where the place was, we asked the bus conductor to let us off at the nearest stop to Belfield. As we eventually stepped off the bus, he told us it was the double green gate at the end of the street. We walked very proudly down the street with our bags, hurleys over our shoulders, and boots hanging from the ends. When we saw the large left hand gate with the letters B E L on it, we proceeded through the turnstiles, still with our hurleys over our shoulders, telling the guy on the turnstiles that we were players on the team. I wondered why he looked at us kind of strangely. We could not find a trace of anyone we even recognized, either supporters or team mates and having waited quite a while, it was then that we got a surprise, when two rugby teams came onto the pitch and started their game. We returned to the main gate to examine the right hand side, and saw that the other half of B E L was V E D E R E. We were in the wrong venue. It took us the rest of the afternoon to find our way back to connect with our bus home. That was my one and only attempt to play officially for the school. Neither of us was selected again.

I tried racing on my University bike, and made a fair fist of it, but it was tough going across the long grass. My running ability was middling and I didn't learn to swim until later years. Having a little taste of golf from Bray days, I began to play it seriously from my Rathcoole appointment onwards. I became a member at Slade Valley and the Curragh. I was also part of a golf society called the Rathcoole Masters. Golf became a summer game for me, and I did shooting during the pheasant season, from November to January. So between the two it meant I had good outdoor activity all year round. I enjoyed shooting for the walk through the fields, watching the dogs scent and set a bird and it often happened, that we'd walk all day and never fire a shot. It was most enjoyable to be in commune with nature.

My interest in playing far more golf, even in winter conditions, eventually superceded the shooting and today I do very little of the latter. My handicap went from eighteen to eleven and at present I'm at twelve and steady. I always hoped to reach single figures, but never did. I never won a major in a golf club, such as captain's or president's prize, but at the same time I did win quite an amount of glassware and silver in singles which I'm proud to display today. I had an official hole-in-one for which I got a little trophy. But to date, the best thrill I've had was winning a monthly medal, which means playing singles/strokes off the back stakes. My sixty-seven nett just about got there on the back nine. There are many amusing golf stories and I could go off on a tangent here but I must tell you of the fellow who went out in a four-ball and had never played golf in his life before, but he was a keen hurler. He actually had to ask on the first tee, what he was supposed to do. He was told that he should try to hit the ball near to the green three hundred yards away. With his hurling skill and strength, he put the ball on the green with one blow. When everyone had reached the green, the beginner again asked, what he was supposed to do now and was duly told he should try and put the ball in the little hole where the flag was. His reply was, "Why didn't ye tell me that back on the tee." Or like the seasoned caddie when he was asked by the lady American golfer who had already taken twelve shots and hadn't yet reached the green. "What should we do now caddie?" He replied, "I think at this stage Maam, we should conceive."

Golf for me has always been a great means of relaxation and just getting away from the daily routine. Sometimes, in tight competition, the tension can be far from relaxing, but that's all part of the game. While I always go out to win, and only sometimes succeed, at the same time, win or lose, I have a strong mental approach not to let either way bother me too much. I've seen people break clubs over their knees, and I decided if I ever did that, I'd give up the game. It's surprising the effect the game has on some players. I saw a cartoon once, where a little boy watching his dad's face twisted in anger after missing a shot, asked his mother, "Why does dad play a game that makes him mad?" The dad was heard to say at one stage, "I've no problem with the woods, it's getting out of them that's the problem." There's the Heavenly story about golf, where this man prayed very hard that God would let him know if there were golf courses in Heaven. He eventually got his reply directly from "head quarters," which said, "I've good news and I've bad news for you. The good news is, yes, there are golf courses in Heaven. The bad news is, that you're on the first tee in the morning."

Our family home became a golf driving range which we all ran together for ten years and then we sold it and divided the returns between us. During that time a nephew of mine rose to professional ranks and through him, I met and played with a lot of professionals in the game and that was a great thrill and honour. As we picked golf balls on the driving range, I often thought back on the days we picked potatoes in the same fields. In recent years I really like taking a golf holiday away or at home. While nothing major has been achieved in my golfing career, I've enjoyed the game and all that goes with it, and still do today, and hopefully will, for many years to come.

Having developed a love for house plants and learning by mistakes mostly, I put my little background experience from the farm to use, by taking an interest in the gardens of the presbyteries where I lived. In some cases it would take a lot of work to get the place to the stage of even being presentable, and then I would put my own particular shape on it, front and back. I got a bad run of successors in the gardening department, where many of them would have no interest in such things and it would be let go wild. In one place I had the back converted into a putting green and had competitions for the local children. My successor dug it up and sowed potatoes in it. I landscaped the front of another and those who followed put concrete down to make room to park another car. And in a country area I put a lot of work into a garden area that must have been a quarter of an acre, and actually won a prize for it from Bord Failte, and, the successor let it go wild. So all I can say, is that at least I left them in good order and that's as far as I could go.

I also developed over the years a desire to try and put atmosphere into the house where I live. I like it bright and welcoming, so that if and when people came to visit or on parish business, they would find a warm and hopefully colourful house to come to. I discovered if one had only a lamp lighting in the corner of a room and nothing else, you had atmosphere. So lamps and subdued lighting became a feature of mine and for an unknown reason I took a fancy to clocks of all shapes and sizes. The stock builds up when people find out one likes these things, and so I got presents galore of what I obviously liked. Anytime I go to a store where they sell lamps or clocks, I'm sure to come out with one or the other to add further to the selection.

Over the years I've had house-keepers of all shapes, sizes and ages, some in the early days were live-in and in latter years, the daily or casual became the better and sometimes the only available option. They always had their work cut out when it came to dusting and cleaning all the little "knick-knacks." I can cook a simple meal for myself but was never great at house cleaning, washing or ironing clothes. Shopping, I never liked. As a result of all this, I developed the habit of eating out frequently, at least for the main meal of the day, and just having the morning and evening repast at home.

I tried my hand at many musical instruments, beginning with the mouth organ, the deuce harp, the keyboard, the fiddle, the accordion, and the guitar, but never became good at any one of them. However I did have a great urge to create music from an instrument and that's why I always loved live performances and even when listening to music of an orchestral nature, I let my mind drift away as I imagine all the different instruments being used to produce a particular sound. I like all kinds of music and song, but I would have a more sustained interest in the light classical area. I have recordings of the lighter sides of Mozart, Handel, Vivaldi, Bach, and the later musical arranger, James Last. I have no doubt, that as in prayer, music has a profound effect on the mind and body. When I sit back at home or in the car and listen to some favourite piece, which I might seek out for a particular purpose, my mind and body become completely absorbed in a different world. One of my favourite pieces, when I'm in bad form and want something to cheer me up, is the "March of the Hebrew Slaves," by Verdi from Nabuko. I am always uplifted and find peace of mind in this piece whether it is the orchestral or choral version. No matter how independent one might seem to be, everyone needs a little of what's called TLC at some stage in life, and a person who has a liking for certain soft and soothing types of music, can be comforted, uplifted, or calmed, by listening to their favourite pieces. In church of course, song and music play such an important role, and create an atmosphere and an environment conducive to prayerful listening and talking to God. If a live choir, folk group or musician is not available, I have found that recorded music over the public address system, is a good replacement. I've discovered that in all these matters, it's impossible to please people all the time.

One of the great problem areas helped by hobbies and pastimes in this profession, is the loneliness that goes with it. Some occupational therapy or escape would always have been, at least for me anyway, a means of dealing with periods in life where I'd find it really lonely in the house, among a crowd of people, on the altar or in the car. Resorting to alcohol or smoking was only a temporary solution, and in fact by their very nature made the problem worse. The need for interests outside of the ordinary run of things was necessary for personal development in the physical, mental, emotional, and spiritual areas of my life. The loneliness was and is something I've never really got used to, but I've learned to cope with it in a variety of ways under the headings of this chapter.

The concern, support and welfare of my superiors was always there, but very often too far removed to benefit the individual in immediate personal need. Support from fellow clergy and class mates has been of great value. Coming together for a meal and a chat as we do several times each year, has always been a great source of solidarity, as we talk of experiences, and problems at personal and parish levels. These gatherings were known as class conferences in the early days when some guys took it very seriously by getting in a guest speaker to talk about some topical issue of the day, but this soon disappeared and the get-together became a meal, a few drinks for those who indulged, maybe a game of cards, for those who could stay up late, but mostly a means for consolidating the class and trying to look after one another.

While taking some form of relaxation or exercise, I always preferred to couple it with doing something useful or helpful. But if circumstances would not allow, I would at least attempt to find time for a walk somewhere. Not only did I find that this fulfilled my needs but also it allowed great space to think and reflect. If I'm trying to prepare a talk or homily, I seldom write or use any notes if at all possible, and it's during a walk that I can best put together the words that I need for a particular occasion. If the place selected is near fields or woods, then, all the different aspects of nature give great food for thought and even a commune with God Himself. I am always absorbed in features such as rivers, trees, bird and animal life, the skies in all varieties, and the many other interesting things to be found by looking around. Sometimes for me it's great to get away from people for a while, but there's always the chance of meeting some one who knows me or think they know me. Like one little lady I met who said, "Thare yare Father, whare ya now?"

# CHAPTER SEVEN

## THE PRIESTS SHOW AND ME

I would never lay claim to being an actor or a singer, but I would lay some small claim to being in my own way a type of entertainer. While I always liked music and singing very much, I had no particular talent in those fields, although I did try my hand at both, among other things. It was a couple of years into college life, when I discovered at a debate gathering one night, that I was able to make people laugh. It was a funny story about a happening that very day, and it meant mimicking another student, not in an offensive manner I might add, but merely recalling an incident at recreation time and whatever way I re-lived the event for those around, it received a huge laugh and applause. This gave me for the first time in my life, a sense of great satisfaction, that I was able to make people laugh, and furthermore totally on my own initiative. I then felt less inhibited at standing up when I felt like it and just saying what I wished to say. Often when walking with one or two friends I furthered my practice by recalling many childhood funny incidents all to the delight and entertainment of the company. Students were always ready for the story that no one would tell to his mother, however, without being prudish about those type of so-called funny stories, I genuinely never did like searching out the smutty, little meaty ones, because I was beginning to realize even at that early stage, that there were very many funny happenings in real life that when adapted, were very entertaining. That's not to say for one minute that I never told the risky ones, I did, but I didn't seek them out as the only ones available. I could see too at this stage that when presenting any message, be it to a congregation or an audience, with an attractive funny incident maybe at the beginning, middle or end, it could lift those listening to me. During the subsequent years at college, I practiced as much as I could and tried to develop an easy-to-listen-to style of talking to people, whether in public or in private. I learned by sheer grit and determination by not refusing any invitations or offers I received to get up in front of a crowd and do my party piece, and that's all it was at that point. Even if this meant dying the death on the odd occasion, well that was all part of the tough grind it took to develop the ability to mould an audience into the palm of one's hand. I had by now dabbled with and learned a few chords on the guitar and so, with a store of suitable gags in the bag and the ability to bang out a few sing-a-long numbers with my own guitar backing, I had in fact put together a little act of my own that enabled me to be sought after as one who could contribute to any of the functions I attended during the course of my work.

It was in 1976, about midway through my Rathcoole stint, that I got a phone call one day to know if I'd help by joining a group of priests from the diocese that very evening at a fund-raising show for a fellow priest who had just been informed earlier that same day that the professional artist who was billed and booked for the show, was not able to appear that night. The show was set for a cabaret house, called the "Hitching Post" on the Maynooth Road from Dublin. Obviously word had got around that I had gained some reputation as one having a good party piece to offer. Other members of the group were similarly summoned at the last minute, to try and get this unfortunate hard-working fellow priest out of an awful spot. The six hundred capacity house was already sold out with only the resident band on stage but not the artist who had been advertised, and so after the rather embarrassed priest explained to his audience that the person they all came to hear would not be appearing, he hopefully (and I'd say prayerfully) told them that he had a group of fellow priests who were all entertainers in their own right, and they were going to do the show. There were ten of us who had never played together before, never met the band present to do the backing, and did not know from Adam what each fellow was going to attempt to perform on the stage. Anyway after nearly three hours of non-stop song, comedy and music, the audience was absolutely delighted with their night out, and many people asked afterwards where and when we were doing such a show again, not knowing that we had just come together that very evening for the first time. That's how the "All Priests Show" began and the rest is history, as they say.

The first few shows were very tentative with one of our group doing the M.C. and link-man, and as each band we played with was different, it made the question of intro-music and suitable levels in pitch, difficult for us to put it all together as a smooth running show, also the fact that no rehearsals were made possible. Despite all the teething problems, our M.C. became our manager and many bookings and requests began to flow in. It took a little time to get the balance of singers, musicians, and comedians worked out, but by sheer repetition, and learning from many experiences, a nice free-flowing two and half hours of family entertainment came together, with something for everyone. There was rock and roll, country and western, ballads, classical, instrumentals, and of course comedy, which was my contribution with help from one or two others who also did their own style of comedy presentation.

As the show settled into at least once a week, Thursday was agreed to be the most suitable night for all concerned and I slotted into the final act of the evening and also did what they called "the wrap up." I was constantly seeking out new and suitable gags for the act. After every show, many well-meaning people would offer their contribution by making me listen to an often long-winded story they thought would do for my act. Sometimes these would be quite smutty and they'd say, "Clean that up now and you'll be able to use it next time." For a lot of them, the cleaning up would in fact need major reconstruction. My own method was looking out for real life situations that were in themselves funny, then in many cases, personalizing them, as if I had been actually implicated in the event, and so I'd present it by saying that this particular funny incident happened to me, today, yesterday, or whenever. I watched and listened to some of the great masters of comedy, on television and radio, and picked up many tips and techniques of how to work an audience. The one absolute and most important ingredient of telling a joke to people, is timing. This timing is located within the punch-line of what's funny in the story. This can only be achieved by practice and very often, learning from mistakes. There is no doubt also that a lot depends on the type of audience, the venue, the sound system, the number of people, the mix of age levels, the county or country one might be in. So for these and many other reasons, I had to build up quite a stock of gags whereby I'd be able to select certain themes, or approaches with stories that suited the place and people of that show. It became a great comfort to know that if one line of attack was not working, I had alternative material. The question often asked also, was "How do you remember them all?" Having listened and learned, I blocked mine into groups by telling four or five about shops, doctors, buses, pubs, children, confessional, church, and so on. Quite a lot of the stories I often used in homilies when they suited the subject in hand.

I'm sure you're wondering when I'm ever going to give you a few examples. I was always told that a good start and a good finish is important. Church-related confessional ones I always found got immediate attention particularly from an Irish audience. The man who had not been to confession for many years, decided he'd make an effort because of a family wedding. He went into the church, straight to the box where he knew the priest was waiting, and without looking up or opening his eyes, he just pressed his nose against the wire grid, unleashed a litany of woe, lasting several minutes and in such a flow that he seemed not even to break for breath. Then with a big sigh of relief, he raised his head, opened his eyes and looked through the grid, only to find that there was no priest there at all. But he could see across to the opposite cubicle where another penitent was also waiting, and he simply said to him, "Where's the priest?" The fella across the way said, "I don't know, if he heard what I just heard, I'm sure he's gone for the police." An old priest who loved chatting to people in the confessional, would always ask what the person worked at, whether they were married, if they had a family and so on. On asking this man one night some of these questions, he got the answer, that he worked for the circus and was an acrobat. The priest said he'd never seen an act of that sort. The man invited him to come out of the box, sit down and he'd give a little demonstration in the church which seemed empty at the time. So as the acrobat did his various stunts on and over the seats, neither he nor the priest saw the two elderly ladies down at the back watching all this carry on, and one said to the other, "Mary if that's the penance we're gettin' I'm not goin' in there." I would often try a couple like that for an opening and judge by the reaction whether to stay in that vein for a while or to immediately move in another direction. This might take two or sometimes more attempts to get the feel of the audience and then maybe having settled them down and made my decision I would branch off into another set.

At the presentation of a particular show, the time factor for each act depended on how many were available on a given night. If there was the full compliment of around eight, then four and four, first and second halves, would have about twelve minutes each. If we were short of acts, the compere would say to me as I went on stage, you have all the time in the world, give them "the kitchen sink." Over the years as I look back on my repertoire of jokes, I would divide them into the best to the worst; the ridiculous to the sublime; and the "risque" to the child-like. When I use the word "risque" that would be very mild in the light of what we see and hear today. Some of the early agricultural true stories I had used were frowned on by some of my colleagues and they'd express a voice of disapproval. I never thought in a rural area at anytime that they would harm or shock in anyway. Judge for yourself. A farmer who had a pig was hoping to put her in the family way and the nearest farmer with whom he was friendly was just a quarter of a mile down the road, where there was a male. He was told to bring the sow down but in order to treat her gently, better to carry her in a wheel barrow. After the service in the neighbouring farm, he was loading her back into the wheel barrow and having paid for the service rendered, he asked how he would know whether it was successful or not. So the older and more experienced farmer said, watch her first thing in the morning and if she's rolling in the mud, that's a sure sign she's happy and with pig. But if she's eating grass, better bring her back again. The first morning she was eating grass, into the barrow and down again; the second morning, eating grass, into the barrow and off again, and the third the very same. The farmer was getting fed up at this stage and said to the wife, "You get up there and look out the window and see what she's doing this morning." His wife stood looking out the window and said nothing. He retorted, "Come on good woman, tell me, is she eatin' the grass again," and she said, "No." "Well then is she rollin' in the mud?" And again she said, "No." "Well then what is she doing?" The wife answered, "She's sittin' in the wheel barra."

The same pig farmer very often came home late and drunk and the wife got fed up with all this and so one night as he arrived home in the usual state, she would not even allow him into the bedroom; instead she told him to go off and sleep with the pigs, because that's where he really belonged, she felt. He was so out of his mind, he quietly obeyed and went to the shed and lay down beside the sow on the straw. When he awoke the next morning, with his arm around the sow, he thought he was in his bed with the wife, and, he said, "I'm married to ya now, it must be twenty or thirty years, and I never knew ya had buttons on yer night dress." It's true there are various types of jokes. An example of a rather childish one is the man who stopped his dog from the non-stop barking by giving it a good kick. He was wearing "Hush Puppies." Or the ridiculous, i.e. when the optician said to his patient, "I knew you needed glasses, when you came in through the window, instead of the door." The sublime, i.e. when the Pope started Mass in Irish and two curious fellas attending thought he was going to say the whole thing in Polish. There are bad jokes too which sometimes you could get away with, depending on the audience; like the fellow who asked for a dozen nails, and the attendant asked "How long do you want them?" and he said, "I'd like to keep them."

In the early years of the show, it was really tough work having to play with different bands everywhere we went. After a number of bad experiences, for instance being presented with a teenage pop group as our backing, a ceili band, or maybe as happened, on a couple of occasions, nothing at all. The no band at all happened for the first time down in Cork and the organizers said when asked about the band, "Shure we thought yee shmart fellas from Dublin would have yeer own band." So to make things easier we eventually set up our own band having agreed with them to play every Thursday. Then when we began to tour in Ireland or abroad, they would come with us, and bring along sound and lighting. Things became relaxed and the show was more enjoyable for us and of course consistently professional in its presentation. We toured the four corners of Ireland in the early eighties and I have some good videos I made myself of those trips and the fun we had on and off the stage. I set up the first English Tour which was for about ten days to the cities with large Irish populations and we did the first couple travelling over by boat and everywhere by train and taxi. An agency eventually organized these trips more efficiently and got us into the big venues of England, Scotland and Wales. We often shared tours with people like,

Paddy Reilly, Brendan Grace, Johnny McEvoy, Susan McCann, The Bachelors, and would you believe fronting us one night was a shy young singer named Daniel O'Donnell. All of these were lovely people, and I got to know them very well. I had a phone call one night from Boston from Eily Patterson, Frank's wife, to know if I and a few of the lads from the show would be interested in taking up a regular tour contract that Frank had been doing for years in the Boston/New York area. I put it together and so started the American trips that lasted for many years. The U.S. and U.K. tours were nearly always in March and would of course include St. Patrick's Day.

We had just finished a good night's show in Jury's Hotel one night, when an Irish-Australian asked if we would be interested in travelling to the cities of Queensland and from there around to the States. I thought there was no substance behind this. I told him to write to me and put on paper what he had in mind. To my surprise, he did write soon after and his plan was to set up big venues in Brisbane, Melbourne, Sydney, then to San Francisco, Chicago, Denver, Washington, and finally to New York to play Carnegie Hall. Six of us agreed to do this and we were flown out first class, met and transported everywhere in stretched limos; we also stayed in top class hotels. It was a marvellous trip, especially finishing in the famous Carnegie Hall.

The priests show has been on the go for twenty-four years and I was with the group up to 1999 after doing twenty-eight years of gigging myself since 1972. While the show has served a tremendous service in many departments, I feel at this stage it has about run its course, and has very much served its purpose in its own way and in its own time. Nothing lasts forever. I was delighted to have been with the show since its beginnings and I enjoyed the experience of the show business world as a result. It also meant travelling around the world, appearing on T.V. and radio, and being the centre of media hype in many places we visited. We were privileged to appear on many BBC and RTE presentations, such as ITV, Barrymore, Liam O'Muruchu, The Late Late Show, and others. In addition it was an honour to be involved in making cd's, cassettes and videos. I was really thrilled one night after a show in England, when a couple of spotters from the audience came to me and asked if I would be interested in doing a part on a ten week series with the Frank Carson show. To think that I qualified to be that highly regarded in the comedy world, was to me a huge compliment. Unfortunately I was not a member of "Equity" which was and still is a prerequisite for anyone appearing on such shows, and although I tried all possible means to gain membership, everything failed, and so I could not honour my prize invitation.

Over the years, many members of the group either resigned because of other work pressures, some left the ministry for personal reasons, and some just died. It was always difficult to keep up the panel number to the comfortable ten, as many talented and most eligible priests, did not wish to commit themselves to the once a week show. But despite such struggles we managed to keep a workable group together over the years. I always had a firm decision in my mind as to the rating of the show in my priorities. My priestly ministry was very much the primary, and the show, very much secondary, and so it meant little to me whether the show folded or I had to leave, which I did in the end. Having said that, all the experiences that went with the show were very much complimentary to the work of the pastoral ministry. It meant meeting people from all parts of the world in a social environment. Apart from the fund-raising, the entertainment, the camaraderie of the priest members, it was also excellent P.R. for priest and church. It enabled people to see the priest in a different image. While saying Mass or presenting a ceremony from the altar, is not exactly a show, there has to be certain elements of presentation that enhance the service and very often the stage experience has helped me in that area. Whether on the stage or on the altar, I would never be up there just to gain personal admiration, but rather to present a message either as entertainment or prayer, to the people present, in a happy and interesting manner and thereby keep their attention on what was taking place.

Personally, I've been most grateful for the bond of friendship which was solidly established among the priests and the generous and sincere backing on and off the stage from the three exemplary laymen in the band which was maintained all over the years. I felt the honour of meeting so many great people among the organizers, the audiences, those who slogged tirelessly at promoting and selling our merchandise as in brochures, tapes, videos etc. For all the Irish shows, the organizers looked after the funds raised from the night. They just booked the show, arranged a venue, secured our band (whom they paid) and then just sold their tickets. We never handled or received any money. The small returns from the merchandise helped the group with travelling expenses, a meal out together occasionally, and for secretarial and postal needs. The amount raised in this country for a variety of charities has now topped six and a half million Punts. The funds raised on foreign trips were distributed at the discretion of the agencies to the local needs of the town or city in which we played.

I think, looking back, that "The All Priests" show has been a phenomenal success and while it will always be remembered by so many people all over the world, I feel a personal pride and sense of satisfaction at having been part of it for so long. Perhaps it can best be summed up in the words of Ralph Waldo Emerson, when he said about life, "To laugh often and much; to win the respect of intelligent people and the affection of children; to earn the appreciation of honest critics and endure the betrayal of false friends; to appreciate beauty, to find the best in others; to leave the world a little better whether by contented people, an improved building or a redeemed social condition; to know even one life has breathed easier because you have lived. This is the meaning of success."

# CHAPTER EIGHT

## APPOINTMENTS PART II

***Rathcoole***

By 1972 most of the family had settled into their way of life. My two sisters had joined the Cross and Passion Order and there were only a couple of my brothers left at home. It was a trait in our home that my father didn't like the girls leaving and wanted them to stay at home, while my mother wanted the boys to remain. I suppose it was a typical Irish way of thinking. Anyway in March of that same year, I was recalled from London and asked to take up a curacy in Rathcoole, which was originally a small village, cut off by the dual carriage-way in the sixties and then developed into quite a town of over a thousand families. It was part of the parish of Saggart which also included Newcastle, Brittas and Crooksling Hospital. In the seventies, Newcastle became a parish in its own right and that lightened the work load considerably.

When I arrived, the only possessions I had were the car I was driving, a Ford Corsair, (I had come up in the world!), a rocking chair and whatever clothes I had at the time. I was also in debt to the enormous sum of £700, which was a lot of money, to me at least, in the seventies. The house I was moving into was a big old barracks of a place, originally built as a presbytery for two priests and two house-keepers. But the building was a disaster from the beginning because it appears it was built on an underground stream which meant both gable ends sank, splitting the main walls on either side. The solution agreed for this was to put two large RSJS' right through the attic of the house being held at either end by a big cross-like piece of steel, and with two large crosses now on each gable end, people thought that was to indicate that it was a priest's house. They did not know the real truth of the matter. I was allotted two rooms on the ground floor, plus bathroom and toilet. There was also accommodation for a live-in housekeeper on the same floor, if required. The other priest who had been there for many years, had the same self-contained apartment upstairs but he had not done anything to the place for a long time.

The entire building was in serious need of refurbishing. The large dining room on the bottom floor, with the wall paper falling off, was for common use. It was the custom when a priest was leaving to move to another parish, to take everything with him, and I mean everything. The only thing left in my two rooms was the phone on the floor. There were no curtains, carpets, not even a bulb in the light socket. It reminded me of the man who was removing wallpaper from his front room and when asked by a neighbour if he was decorating, he said no, he was moving. I did not have a spoon to my name. The place was freezing cold. A priest colleague heard of my plight and brought me an old two-bar electric heater to try and improve the air in the place. An older brother bought me a couch which could convert into a bed; it reminded me of my first days in Bray. In those twelve years, things had not improved all that much regarding accommodation. Until I was able to build up my own stock of requirements, I was totally dependent on the other man upstairs. Today, a priest arriving in a similar situation, would not move in until the place was put in order.

It was at this stage that my experience with my father dabbling in furniture, came into its own and with a debt already hanging over me, I had to sink deeper to enable me to furnish and acquire all the usual household things that I needed. Having bought my basic needs in and around the city, I then began to go further afield and dabble in buying and selling bits of furniture. I saw this as a means of clearing my debt of £800. I was determined to be independent and pay this off on my own and in my own way. This sort of bartering would have been very much frowned on by my authorities, but it was the only way I knew of managing on my own. I was delighted to have cleared the debt in one year. But the trading didn't stop there. As other needs arose, such as changing my car, going on holidays, golf club membership etc. I carried on raising funds, because I was absolutely determined not to fall back into debt again, and thank God I never did. I developed a liking for and a little knowledge of antiques, and so often travelled to different parts of the country to auctions and various sources where I'd pick up bits and pieces. I was by no means an expert but I could distinguish between what was the genuine article and what was a reproduction.

There was a huge garden at the back of this house, almost an acre in size and apparently in former years a priest in residence was a fruit and vegetable garden enthusiast and so had the place well stocked with apple trees, raspberry and gooseberry bushes and vegetables of all sorts. He was regularly seen walking down the village with a barrow full of farm yard manure which he would have got locally, and the resident layabouts would be heard to chime in a jeering tone, "There goes Cocko (that's what they called him) with his barra o' shit." After he moved on, the garden went into a state of neglect, taking on the appearance of a dense jungle. Nobody had shown any interest in doing anything with it. The other priest's house-keeper used to keep some ducks and apart from the mess they created, they were certainly no help in improving conditions at the back. I had no real desire to tackle the rear but I did keep the grass in control at the front.

This appointment was thoughtful in many ways, with my parents still going strong, and I only about five miles from home. I also had the advantage of already knowing quite a few people from early childhood when we'd come to this village in the pony and trap. With many new-comers in the then developing areas there was the usual slow process of the old residents trying to integrate with the new. For many newly married couples and young families, this area of Rathcoole seemed a very long distance from the city. I heard one newly arrived lady say, "I'm out in the country here, I'll never see me Ma again." But it quickly became a mere suburb of Dublin city.

The building of the final phase for that period was coming to a close when I arrived and it meant that the vast majority of the new comers were all in the same boat, trying to settle and become part of the place. There was immediate pressure on our schools and an extension was quickly completed, bringing it to a seventeen teacher school. But I sensed a terrific need for community spirit and some means of bringing people together. Plans were well underway to build a community centre and a site had already been purchased. The nearest church was either Saggart or Newcastle, a few miles away in opposite directions. A special mass bus provided a Sunday morning service to ferry people to and from the various masses and it did the rounds every Sunday up to lunch time. I had no doubt that a church in Rathcoole was a priority and would help greatly in bringing people together. I could identify with the new comers, because I was also trying to re-adjust and settle back to Irish life style after the hectic run in London. So my needs in trying to find roots as it were, was an advantage to me in many ways, because in speaking to people, I saw very clearly that their needs were so similar to my own. So there was a great sense now of everybody working together for the common good and very soon I could see great potential for community development.

I have no doubt that the Good Lord was working in and through the events that followed. It happened that the largest building company, had built a substantial prefabricated block of offices, and expected to be in the area for quite a few years to follow. The demand for houses quickly fizzled out and building came to a standstill. So these builders were left with this relatively new, though temporary, block of offices. It was in very good shape with about fifteen different rooms. One of the directors contacted me to inquire if it would be useful, for a youth club or the like. Our youth club was already operating in the old school and the young people were quite happy there. Anyway I did not think that this prefab was suitable for use as a youth club. When I took a close look at the building and visualized it with all the partitions taken out, I thought it could be used as a church. One thing followed another very quickly and these people were looking for an immediate decision. As the parish priest was away at the time, I had to go it alone. So I went straight to their head office in Dublin and made a deal to buy the building and have it renovated to an open plan which would hold five hundred people. The cost of the building including the renovation, making it ready for use as a church, was £8,000. It went on record as the cheapest church ever made available in the Diocese. As the builders did not wish to part with the actual site at that time, in case building in the area would begin again, they gave us a free lease for at least five years and then with an option to buy. We did buy it for a very nominal sum a few years later. When the P.P. returned, I told him to sit down, I had news for him. I informed him that we had a church in Rathcoole. His mouth remained wide open for a long time. But he went along with everything and we opened officially on December 8th about the year 1975. While the building naturally deteriorated quicker than a permanent building, despite a few leaks here and there, and, almost being burned down by a fallen candle, still it actually served as the church for twelve to fourteen years. During those years, plans were going on to acquire a site and build a new and permanent church. It became very popular and people loved it for its intimacy and simplicity and when the time came eventually to move, they didn't want to leave it. The desired aim and object was widely achieved in bringing the community together through the medium of the church and the Christian message. I remember one Sunday a lady with a large family came running back after Mass in a state, "Did anybody see a child around anywhere, I left one behind." I had the little fellow in the sacristy. He was so young, he didn't even know his own name.

The entire community pulled very well together and by now had a site and plans in place for a community centre. I realized there was another site available nearby and possibly suitable for a new church. I suggested selling the big old house where the two of us priests lived and buying two smaller ones out in the community. We sold the property for £22,000, and with that bought two other houses, the site for the new church, and even had £4,000 over for savings. There was a recession at this time, so we sold and bought at a very low rate. I was involved in getting a day-care centre up and running and was lucky to acquire an old ambulance from the health board to ferry the elderly around and bring them to the centre. I got great value out of it. I left the word "Ambulance" on it, and I was hoping to have the blue flashing lights and siren also, but that was not allowed. I'm happy to say this centre is still flourishing today with full time staff and a new mini bus.

It was at this stage I became interested in house and outdoor plants. I was in a house one afternoon and saw these little sprigs of something in a jam pot. The lady told me she was rooting some busy lizzies which I had never heard of and neither had I seen this procedure before. She gave me one to try it and soon my house was full of them. I was in a farmhouse on a visit and saw lovely little white puppies running around. I was fascinated by them and the woman of the house asked me if I'd like one. I could not refuse and picked out a male, white and brown in colour. I put it in my overcoat pocket and off I went. Little did I think I'd be coming home that evening with a dog. He was a cross between a Jack Russell and a poodle. Next morning, totally out of the blue a lady arrived at my door very sad because her little dog had just been killed on the road and wished to get rid of its lead which was in fact a straddle type holder with a metal name tag attached. I now had a dog, a straddle lead, and even though it was a male, I still gave him the name on the strap i.e. Kim. I became very attached to this little lad and had him for twelve years.

It was in the early seventies one Sunday afternoon that the Club House of Slade Valley Golf Club exploded, injuring several people but miraculously, killing no one. It was caused by natural gas leaking through the building and then a naked flame set it off. We were extremely lucky because the night before we had a parish function there with nearly three hundred people, and surely if it happened then there would have been fatalities. The fund-raising went on relentlessly and I enjoyed all the sessions that went with it. There were many celebrities living in the actual parish at that time and I got to know them very well. I managed to get at least a verbal agreement from them all to appear on the one bill in a monster once-off effort to be held in Dublin's Olympia Theatre, at £10 a head, with the line up including, The Chieftians, The Wolfe Tones, Paddy Reilly, Frank Patterson and Brendan Grace. It would no doubt have been a sell out, but I was now coming up to my tenth year in the place, and I must say I enjoyed the whole period of growth, participation and learning what it was like working in a real parish; I was then changed to a city parish, and the big event never materialized. For me this appointment was most fulfilling as my first real contact with people in a home parish and I must say I found uprooting to leave was traumatic. While I had a few "firsts" to my credit, like plant life, dogs, gardening, another first of a rather sinister nature was beginning to take hold of me without my recognizing it nor acknowledging it, and that was the consumption of alcohol. I was consuming more than I should and it certainly was beginning to affect my life, my health, and my work. If I was confronted at the time, I would have been in total denial that any problem remotely existed. A separate chapter will outline the sequence to this.

The Rathcoole appointment of ten years was the longest one I had done to date and while the entire community grew with me, I also in a very significant way grew with them. When I eventually moved to a nice semi-detached house in a small estate, I became and felt far more integrated not only with my immediate neighbours but with the parishioners as such. The children around me practically lived in and around my door and house. I had a most beautiful, happy and friendly relationship with them and that went for all the children in the school also. They minded the phone, manned the door, took Kim for walks, and hugged and kissed him sometimes more than I had time to do. Looking back on those years, I was so lucky to be able to experience the warmth and love of children, but in the light of the many subsequent scandals in the church, no priest, no matter how special he may think he is, can in anyway, be over familiar with children or young people in any department of his ministry. In schools or in church or anywhere children assemble, great care and absolute discretion must be maintained. The children I got to know so well in the school and around the parish, but particularly in the neighbourhood, I know had a great regard and love for me, and I thank the Lord for the privilege of tasting a little of His love, through them. I felt so sorry for one little girl whom I baptized and was with her for her Confirmation, on the day I was moving, she sat on the nearby wall for the day and just cried. I cried too, for her and many more. Making her Confirmation around that time was Michelle Smith.

I always had people around the place, in the car, and in the mini bus when I got it. I was a regular driver for the senior citizens taking them to the day centre. Both bus and car had tow bars and I was constantly borrowing trailers to haul a variety of things here and there. In many ways I had become part of the place and the people and felt quite comfortable. I was also a familiar figure at functions, weddings, ballad sessions and was a regular with the lads having a pint of Guinness. But so much of that began to get a grip on me and many dangerous chances would have been taken by driving with much above the limit on board. I remember myself and a colleague were sitting in the car outside a certain hostelry chatting after a late-night drink, it must have been at least 2am when a police car pulled up along side us and asked what we were doing hanging about at that hour of the morning. I was sitting in the driver's seat and did the speaking as I said, "Have you fellas nothing better to do than interrupt two clergymen discussing the business of our parishes no matter what time of the night it is, or where it is either?" I was politely answered by the one who said, "We're sorry for interrupting the good work Fathers. Good night now and safe home." We should have been arrested and put in jail and that's what would happen today.

The day-today life as the local curate still had a touch of the traditional about it. There was the daily and Sunday masses and confessions, visiting the house-bound, sick calls, the schools, and responding to many kind invitations to lunch or evening meals with families, and there were many such hospitable people around. Sick calls were still part of the life then, either to a house or a road accident. There were many serious and far too many fatal accidents on the dual-carriage way and I witnessed many horrifying scenes to which I was called. Today the priest is seldom called out on a sick call, and I'd say never to a road accident anymore. It has gone from one extreme to the other, because I remember an old lady who was living alone, phoned me at 2.30am one morning to tell me that her cat had died and with it her whole world had caved in. She was one who had the priest on her mind for everything. While I did not go out that night, I did call to see her next day. About the same time on another morning, I was called to the upper and hilly part of the parish to where an old man was dying and when I arrived, there was a good drinking session in full swing in the form of a wake, and the poor man was not yet dead, but very close to it. As I attended him, no one else came into the room, and when finished I was invited to join in the drinking, which I declined. All were now happy that "He's had the priest with him," and that was regarded as the most important. I knew the man would not see the night through, and as I left, the lady of the house, the dying man's wife asked me, "Do you think should I get the doctor?"   So deaths and funerals were very much part of the regular work in the church and with the families. I had more baptisms than weddings, but the latter increased as time went on.

The "All Priests Show" was a very good means of meeting fellow priests and many people. While the show biz scene did not really add to the drinking scenes, the problem was creeping in through other channels and for other reasons. I was concerned but did nothing about it. I thought nothing of a drinking session during the day. I really believed this was all just good fun and that there was no real obvious reason for drinking other than that, at least so I thought. My mother often visited and began to show concern for my style of life, and would often drop the frequent reminder of her disapproval but I always found some excuse in work or the like. My older sister lived in Toronto at this time and I began to make visits there and many subsequent ones to the various parts of Canada she and her husband moved to. I was still able to hold everything together despite the external and the internal developments, that were taking place.

Being so long in the one place made it difficult to keep any sort of novel approach in the manner of presenting things, because I had run out of all my options. As I was once told, you have one sermon and the rest is just padding; just the same as a singer has one song. There was another man working with me the while I was in the old house and then changes began as I saw three different priests come and go, eventually there was no replacement, and so I was on my own for the latter part of my stay. Except for one, I got on okay with the others and there was co-operation. Sometimes traits of jealousy would cause little rifts when people would ask for me rather than the other guy. This was often embarrassing for me, but I had no real control in many cases. On the whole, team work with fellow curates worked well and the P.P. was simply an "old gent" whom I liked a lot.

In his late seventies my Father was beginning to show signs of not being himself and slowing down very much. He was still quite active, pottering about the place, but of course still smoking. He asked me quietly one day if I could get someone to look at his eyes as his long vision outdoors and all that he enjoyed so much and also his reading which he loved were quite impaired. So I did the big thing, made an appointment with a top specialist in Fitzwilliam Sq., and brought him in myself. He did not want any fuss from the family. As the ophthalmologist was putting him through his paces by changing lens in a master frame fitted over his eyes and asking him to read the letters and figures on the hanging card, my father said continuously, "No bloody use,………..no bloody use." But all the while the specialist was washing his own original glasses in a special fluid and water. Without saying anything, he just slipped his own glasses back on and got the immediate response, "Bloody great …….bloody great." He then read the card down to the smallest letter. The optician said, "Go home and wash your glasses." It was nothing more than a scum on the lens from all the smoking. This whole exercise and simple advice, cost me fifty pounds!

Apart from his sight which was actually very good for his age, he was obviously not well in other ways, and it took a lot of persuasion to get him to agree to see a doctor and even more to get him to agree to have an x-ray and that showed he had a small malignant tumor on his lung and the family (not himself) was told about this. We were told that this could spread either down into the system or to the brain and that he would have roughly another three years. The medical people were very accurate almost to the month, and the effects of the tumor spread up to the head and he soon got to the stage when he could not be left alone and my mother was not able to handle him on her own.

We prevailed on him to try a lovely new nursing home just opened near me in Rathcoole and again with no fuss, I was the one who took him one afternoon and no other member of the family apart from the mother was around so as not to discommode him too much. Never having been to hospital all his life, this move left him completely out of sorts and from his arrival on Friday afternoon to Monday he was completely restless and that night I dropped in to say good night to him to find the local doctor was with him as he had slipped into a coma. Having alerted all the family, there was a day and night vigil until the following Friday when he died at 2am November 12th. 1977, aged 80. This was the first death in the family which made it very difficult. I had the feeling that somehow these people I loved were going to live forever. He was given full honours and a great funeral. The local pipe band played us out of Rathcoole and then as we passed the home place the customary stop was made and it so happened that some extremely helpful person over stacked the fire, and as a result the chimney went on fire. This was always remembered as a final farewell. I felt pain, a deep sense of sorrow, and loss. Even as I express these words right now, I can still feel part of the pain and sorrow because as I recall all the memories, I realize now, more than ever before, how much I was attached to my father and how I inherited many of his qualities and characteristics. I pray to him everyday as I do to the other deceased members of the family.

A few years after my father had died and towards the latter part of my stay in Rathcoole, a most remarkable combination of events occurred one mid-summer weekend. I had a holiday planned to go camping in France and I was due to leave on the Sunday evening to head for Rosslare, pick up some camping gear in Waterford and join up with the rest of the group at the harbour. My tickets, passport and all the necessary car documents, I had locked away securely in my small house safe. I finished my usual Sunday masses, had lunch, and my final duty was to officially open a field sports day in the Brittas area. At 5pm I was packing the final few items into the car and left the documents in the safe until last. When I went to get them, do you think I could find the key? It was just a single, ordinary safe key. I had brought it with me everywhere that day as an extra precaution but after tearing everything apart for over two hours, there was no key to be found. I then retraced my movements for the day, where I had said Masses, places I'd been, including going back to the sports field, but there was no trace of the key. By now it was nearly 9pm and even if I did find it, there was no way I'd make it in time for the sailing. Being a Sunday night, there were no services available to help. So I got in touch with the other members of the party, telling them to go ahead, and perhaps I'd be able to join them in a day or two. All members of my family knew I was due to depart that evening but had no idea of the drama developing. I made no contact with anyone, but just decided to go and have a couple of pints, go to bed and try to figure something out next morning.

At 8am I was awakened by small stones being thrown at my bedroom window and looking out I saw one of my younger brothers with his wife looking up, hoping for a reply. They were greatly surprised to find me there. Their new eight week old baby had just died a cot death and they were greatly distressed. I had no idea what had happened to them and they had no idea of my situation. On the way home from the hospital, the wife said to my brother, "Let's call and tell Eamonn about all of this," but my brother said, "There's no point, he won't be there, he's gone off on holiday." She insisted that they try and, that, combined with the circumstances surrounding my not getting away, could only have been providential. So glad was I to be there for them and to support and help at such a needy time, my predicament faded into the background. We brought the little baby to my house, waked him there, and with the entire family gathered he was buried a couple of days later. If I had gotten away, they would never have found me in time. The Lord was with us all in this time of need.

## The Navan Road

The change from Rathcoole did not come as a very big surprise because I had spent ten years there and perhaps in a way it was a bit too long both for priest and people. It was a big upheaval on all sides and I was not too pleased with the idea of moving to a city parish. The farewells then began and between the big one and the many smaller ones, it must have taken over a week to complete all the functions. The generosity of people always amazes me and I was completely showered with beautiful gifts and good luck gestures. There is an unwritten law that we don't go back to do weddings and funerals or any other important events in people's lives, but there were some I could not refuse and had promised to do some of the things asked of me. It created some disapproval from my successor and the then new P.P. in Saggart. In some cases I persuaded some of them to come to my new parish, but all of this soon fizzled out, nevertheless the memories and the many contacts continue to this day.

My new parish was on the Navan Rd. with the house opposite the church. There was another senior curate and the Parish Priest. By this time new rules regarding house furnishings had come in and all the basics were left in place, like carpets, curtains, light fittings etc. By this time, after all my dealing in the business, I had plenty of all the household needs. I did my own moving with the help of a couple of family members, some trailers, and a horse box. I soon had all my own little effects around the house, and made it homely and welcoming. I never liked anyone to think it was a priest's house by obvious signs on entering, but that it was a home first of all and one I was happy to return to every day, and it so happened that a priest lived there. My mother used to say, "I don't see many holy pictures around the place." I soon did a few things to the garden, front and back and had it near enough to my liking. I was forever making changes inside and outside and that led to variety.

The church across the road was huge, seating two thousand people, and at that time attendance was fairly good. The old traditional pulpit was still in use and the custom was that on Sundays the one on duty would talk at all the masses which was not very satisfactory and so that soon changed. The one saying the Mass would say his own few words. That suited me much better, and despite the vast scene and sea of people, I had by then become more comfortable at conveying my ideas and getting a message across in quite a brief time. My growing experience on the stage with the show was a great asset in this regard and did in fact compliment what I was doing in the church. The old "Please the people syndrome" was still haunting me in many ways, and I suppose affecting me more than I thought, it did not have complete control, but in the back of my mind it bothered me. I was still conscious of people's reaction and of course loved approval and the odd compliment on a Mass or a sermon, but I'd get very upset, if there was any adverse remarks either from the other priests or people. It was no harm to get a few of these and I did, but unfortunately I took refuge in a few extra drinks more often than I should have and that was to bring a problem out into the open for the first time. As mentioned, I'll go into more detail on that in its own chapter.

Behind the church were the two separate primary schools, one girls and one boys, each of about sixteen-teacher size. I was asked to be chairman of the Board of Management for the girls' school, but had regular contact with both. A husband and wife were the principals, he in the boys and she in the girls. With them and all their teachers, there was a great atmosphere and spirit in both schools and that lent itself to excellent communication between priest, teachers and pupils. Next to the schools, the new parish centre had just been completed and this added an exciting dimension to church-related activities. Every parish has a great need of such facilities especially today. Such foresight was there in the U.S. and many continental countries, when actually building the churches. Many of our parishes here are now trying to add these facilities to their already existing buildings.

This area of the Navan Road, on the outskirts of the city, developed after the war years and into the fifties. All the churches of that era were very large, as were the numbers attending then, but these were to present problems later with regard to heating, sound and the drop in numbers. I would say that two thirds of the people in the area were young families moving in from the country, mostly the West, to a city location for their work. Many of the men folk were in the Garda and being tall men, most of their children were also very tall. So I did get the distinct impression from the start that many people in the parish were just TALL. Not that I'm into class distinctions, but I've always heard the people of this area described as upper middle class. There was a lot of parish involvement from all sectors of the community and while the church itself was busy for most of its gatherings, the parish centre was soon buzzing every night, and then for the bigger social functions, the main school hall was used. There were regular ceili nights, musical presentations, like "Fiddler on the Roof," "Joseph and his Amazing Technicolour Dream Coat," "Seven Brides for Seven Brothers," among others. An annual fun-filled competitive event was called, "The Pride of the Parish," where the various estates would perform a full night of entertainment which normally ran for a week, depending on the number of groups taking part, each night the various acts were carefully scrutinized by a professional adjudicator and he or she on the final night would give a decision on which group was "The Pride of the Parish," for that year. All age groups took part from the youngest to the very oldest. I must say I enjoyed being involved in this very much as an overall supporter for all taking part. The entire parish of course was noted for its generosity, and the response to any appeal made for a particular charity or urgent need, was phenomenal.

Apart from all that I had the usual parish duties, like Masses, confessions, sick calls and days on duty. I had a daily housekeeper who had been with my predecessor and stayed on with me for my term there. I also had Kim the dog and he soon got used to the city life and traffic. One house-bound lady I visited was very entertaining in her own way. She was a poet and was always prepared for a long chat, even though she knew I was under pressure to make many other calls on schedule. Her middle aged single daughter lived with her. They were both "Rather….rather…." if you know what I mean, but at the same time very religious, supportive and interested in all that was going on in the parish. The old lady kept telling me that one day I'd be a bishop. That made me feel good at the time, but I'm still waiting! We'll leave that in the hands of the Good Lord. One day there was gloom and doom in the apartment because their budgie had died. I immediately volunteered to get them a replacement, which I did a couple of weeks later. They were delighted with this new green coloured bird as the previous one was blue. It was named on the spot, "Timothy." Their apartment on the third floor was adjacent to and over looked the Phoenix Park, and one lovely summer's morning as I made my usual call, there was devastation because "Timothy" had just flown out the open window into the park. There was little hope of him returning. They put out an urgent request on the national radio network and that afternoon had a call from a lady in Stillorgan, about twelve miles south, to say that a budgie answering the description on the radio had just flown in her window. The daughter was in a taxi immediately and of course recognized Timothy straight away by the identity ring on his leg. The really funny twist to the story is that the lady who found the lost bird was herself named "Mrs. Pigeon."

We had some interesting establishments in the parish. Next to the church was the Papal Nunciature and the Nuncio himself came regularly to the church and we all became quite friendly with him, being invited to many functions at his house. Just down the road was a very large hospital for handicapped run by the French Sisters of Charity and there was good mutual involvement there also. Then a little farther up, was the mother and baby home, which housed and helped young single mothers when having and subsequently trying to decide what to do with their babies. I was chaplain to them and did what I could to help. My London experience was very useful. Next door to this was a home for the elderly and I was chaplain there also. While saying Mass for these people one morning, certain old ladies preferred to finger their Rosary beads during Mass, as they had all their lives, and on offering the sign of peace to be shared this day, one lady preoccupied with her Rosary responded to the person offering her the hand of peace, "Go off outa that, you and yer peace, and let me say me prayers."

The area was well settled by my time there and instead of baptisms being in demand, there were more weddings as many families had reached that stage. The number of funerals was growing rapidly. There was a very good choir and two folk groups, senior and junior, in which I got involved. The senior group stayed together, went on to develop into a musical society. Many marriages evolved from couples meeting within the group. When I had just about settled in there by 1983, my mother who had been ailing for most of twelve months, due to a slow heart beat, now took seriously ill. My two sisters were home from distant lands to be with her. She began to fall a lot for no apparent reason, but in fact we were told these were all mini strokes. I persuaded her to use a walking stick for support, which she did reluctantly. That quickly went to a tripod support, a stick with three legs for stability, and then soon after, all within months, I got her a walking frame and when I asked her if she knew how to use it. She retorted, "Of course I know how to use it, do ya think I'm thick or what?" She went down the corridor of the house dragging it behind her!

Soon after she was in a wheel chair and I was delighted, when, one Sunday afternoon the entire family assembled up the fields to survey the layout of the new golf driving range which was about to be built. My mother joined the viewing from the car and enjoyed the scene, not only of the future developments on hand, but delighting in the company of the entire extended family which was to be for the last time. It was the middle of May and a week later in the early hours of May 17$^{th}$ 1983 she died, aged seventy seven, having survived the father by six years. She was a great mother to all ten of us and a great wife to our father. I loved her very much and greatly admired her rock-solid Faith, devotion to prayer, total unselfish dedication to the family and its welfare. She was given a memorable send off and I was very proud to be part of it for such a wonderful lady. It's interesting to note that the date of my mother's death May 17$^{th}$. was also the date of my ordination. I feel in a way that this may not have been purely by accident, but rather providential, and as my class celebrate our anniversary with a mass, it's very easy to remember also my mother's anniversary. I'm convinced she arranged this herself.

Following on this loss, and towards the latter part of my stay in the parish, two significant developments occurred in my life. One was a deep inner desire to be a family and married person like my brothers; to have a wife and children. The urge was a deep inner instinct trying to pull me into that way of life. I even thought that maybe I would find a more fulfilling kind of life and a deeper happiness and satisfaction of the reproductive nature within me. Now, while I had lots of good and sincere lady friends, as I did everywhere I worked, still I was not involved with any one of them with those thoughts in mind. I suppose it was the challenge of celibacy looming at me and putting me to the test. In ways if I put together the bereavement, the natural urge within, and my own confused background which was never systematically or professionally looked at, I suppose it was no great surprise that I took solace in alcohol again and this time it came to a head, when I had to go for treatment for the first time. After six weeks, I and everybody concerned presumed all was well, and life was great for seven or eight years and then the reality of the ugly monster raised its head again.

While my fellow priests were very generous, kind and supportive, I did feel towards the end of my fifth year there, a strain and tension, that I could have done without. So for the first time in my career, I actually asked for a change, and having expressed a liking for the sea, my wish was soon answered when I was asked to go to a lovely spot in Wicklow, called Kilcoole, in the greater parish of Kilquade, which was on the East Coast right on the sea.

*Kilcoole*
In 1986 I knew a move for me would be in the air that summer and when I got the letter to say I'd been appointed to Kilcoole in the greater Parish of Kilquade, I honestly had no idea where exactly it was, except that it was somewhere down the East Coast. A classmate of mine who was originally from that general area, drove down with me one afternoon to explore the area. The parish is situated on the inner coast road and therefore would not be seen when travelling down the main South East road. That made it all the more attractive but none the less busy, as it was a developing area with many young couples having moved down from the city to find a reasonably priced house and be assured of employment in the local factory engaged in manufacturing refuse sacks which catered for two to three hundred. But unfortunately earlier in that same year, the parent company of the main factory had pulled the plug on their branch in Kilcoole, leaving several hundred people unemployed and feeling stranded way down this coast road. It was a big blow to the whole area and soon after my arrival, I could sense this air of gloom and doom about the place. Commuting to the city by car was about an hour and the Dart to Bray was just being completed at the time. Many families had major decisions to make immediately in order to survive. Quite a few packed up and sold out. But the vast majority stuck it out and although they had to endure a few difficult years, in the end this paid off and these people were glad with the decision they had made to stay, as things improved generally and the small industrial estate developed other smaller ventures giving alternative local employment.
The little bungalow house I moved into was situated across the road from the church and was only five to six years old, in fact some of the builders' residue was still to be found around the house. It had been built on the corner of a greater site used for the new boys school which had been completed at the same time. While it was purpose-built as a presbytery, the garden was left in an open plan situation. There was no landscaping

done, no fencing surround, no pathway to the door, no garage; in fact it was like a tent in the middle of a field and it was left as free-for-all, cattle, horses, dogs, people, children, anybody and anything rambled around the place as on a commons. When I looked up the plans, I could see that fencing, landscaping and the like were planned but never completed at the time. So I decided early on that I would do something about completing that work, which I did over the following couple of years.

The lovely and well-known church was located across the road. Just at that time the T.V. soap, "Glenroe," was beginning to take off and the church and house were featured quite a lot as they continue to be today. The building was a simple but attractive structure seating about seven hundred people and was so different from the huge church of Navan Rd. It was blessed and dedicated by the late J.C.McQuaid and although it would have been planned and designed in pre-Vatican years, the foresight was there to build it in the modern style, with altar and tabernacle situated to facilitate celebrating Mass facing the people. For many years the local people fought hard and fund-raised endlessly to try and build their own church and arrange to have the curate live in the village area, rather than in Delgany, which at that stage had not grown at all. For those years and going back generations earlier, people walked the Mass paths to the church in Kilquade taking about forty five minutes, which was lovely in the summer, but in wintry or wet conditions, was quite a strenuous ordeal. In latter years, a bus service was laid on and the Mass paths like many others in the area became overgrown and inaccessible. But with the advent of local schemes, the increase in tourism, and for historical reasons, this path and many like it all over the country, were uncovered, cleared up and made accessible once again.

From the first day I arrived, I knew I was going to like the parish, the village, the country scene, the sea, but above all, the people who were warm and welcoming. There was quite a similarity between Kilcoole and Rathcoole, in that old and new parishioners were working on integrating and living together. Over time the whole community gelled very well into a lively, happy, active and very enthusiastic Christian family. It had the additional similarity in that Kilcoole was part of a greater parish and in fact must have been one of the largest, certainly the most scattered, parishes in the diocese. In addition to the very old pre-famine church at Kilquade, and the new church in Kilcoole, also included were the church at Newtownmountkennedy, the hospital chapel, the Newcastle Oratory, and the chapel at the Carmelite Convent in Delgany. That meant in all six Mass centres had to be served and with three priests, this was quite a work load.

With the parish priest living in Kilquade, the other curate in Newtown, and myself in Kilcoole, it left us all running our own areas in our own way, and then sharing the other parts between us. The other men were kind hard-working priests and as we met at least once a month there was good co-operative team work which led to a happy environment between us. I was given a free hand more or less, as it enabled me to do my own work in my own way and time. Like anywhere else, it took a couple of years to settle in properly and get to know people better and find out their needs, likes and dislikes etc. Being much further removed from the family home now, it meant that visits home were not as regular as before. Anyway with both parents now dead, the family home was never the same again, but with an older brother and his family now living there, the door is always open and any member of the family is made feel free to enter as always with no need for knocking or formalities. That creates a good spirit and bonding between all the family members and is very much appreciated by all.

What attracted me to this new Christian community was not so much the challenge of doing the work around the house, or realizing the church would need re-roofing, or the usual demands made by the local schools and of course all the other ordinary parish duties that went with the job, but rather, a people and a whole locality that were steeped in history and had worked very hard to emerge from a very one-sided Western British influence for many years. I could see very clearly from the outset when attending either a church service of either denomination (i.e. Church of Ireland or Catholic) or being at a social function, that there was a terrific spirit of mutual understanding and acceptance which again took years of hard work and effort on the part of both sides of the divide. Having been brought up in a very strict and traditional Catholic environment, we were never allowed or encouraged to mix with or enter the churches of people of other persuasions. For the first time in my life, I not only felt comfortable and made welcome to inter-church occasions, but I actually enjoyed it, and it was sharing part of what this entire community had worked so hard at for many long years. I became quite friendly with the local Church of Ireland ministers and the collaboration extended to the clergy in the area also. The six locations of the churches in the parish, had their own distinct and individual characteristics and mentalities. So I found one had to be rather careful and discreet when moving around these unique and distinct communities because each had their own style. This I found fascinating and challenging and made life very interesting in this widespread and vast parish.

The growing popularity of "Glenroe" nationwide and the fact that the Kilcoole community had been chosen as its location, attracted many visitors and tourists to the village. The Druids Glen Golf Club was developing which was to host the Irish Open for a few years and attract more people. I was honoured to celebrate Mass on the course for the final day of the golf each year. The famous seaboard for miles on either side was the scene for many international fishing festivals and the adjoining slob land was home and nesting area to a variety of migrating birds such as the Brent Geese from Canada, and the Terns from North Africa and many others. My mind and body became enveloped in all of that and I learned to appreciate life and nature and all that they have to offer much more than ever before. I could identify with the words of the great George Bernard Shaw when he wrote, "Life is no brief candle to me. It is a sort of splendid torch which I have got a hold of for the moment, and I want to make it burn as brightly as possible before handing it on to future generations."

I soon realized that in just a few years from then, the church would be celebrating its silver jubilee of twenty-five years. This was a great target to motivate the entire community to mark the occasion and of course to have some necessary work done in time. I soon had my house surrounding in good shape and in fact won second prize in the county for best new garden. Work on the roof of the church got underway and was completed in plenty of time. As a matter of interest it cost almost as much to repair the roof as it did to build the entire church. I got an excellent group of men and women together to organize a week of activities in and around the church with something on offer every day and night. It was I feel one of the highlights of my stay in Kilcoole and the week culminated with the entire parish walking all the Mass paths in procession to converge on a Corpus Christi Procession through the village, and finishing up with Mass in the old grave yard down the back of Lott Lane.

Although we had many church-related groups and activities, I was constantly endeavouring to bring the whole parish together more, under an umbrella as it were and to try and create a parish spirit. I tried church events and social functions. I had "The All Priests Show" down a few times and while people said on these occasions how great it was to meet up and see people they hadn't met for ages, still it ended there and all went back to their own separate community or village identity and could not see the wider concept of the parish and its needs. This is not a criticism but a fact of life as it was and no one would or could ever make the parish work on similar principles to that of a city or semi urban community.

A group of nuns were a part of the village for many years and did great work in the schools and community. There's a story, and it's only a story, of the nun waiting outside the local pub where the bus stop was. It was a very cold day and a customer going into the premises asked her if she'd like something to warm her up. She agreed to have a little brandy and she asked if he would put it in a cup. When he ordered the drink and asked for it to be put in a cup the barman said, "Don't tell me that nun's out there again." It's only a story. The better one is about the Dublin lady who came to visit her husband's grave and inquired where a certain Paddy O'Toole was buried. She was told there was only a Maggie O'Toole to be found on the register, whereupon she said, "That's him, everything is in my name."

While I enjoyed a very satisfying period in Kilcoole, and had a very good relationship with people and children in the schools and around, the loneliness factor made its presence felt very often and although eight years had elapsed since my previous crisis, the alcohol problem raised its ugly head again and a second treatment followed. Again, I will give more details later. I was coming close to being promoted to my own parish and possibly even greater, but this was a major setback. As you'll read elsewhere, I bounced back and got terrific support from the people and went on to enjoy another couple of years there to bring me up to eleven in all. Despite the hiccups there was a great sense of good will in the entire community. Having been there for so long, they thought I was there forever, but the time did come when I was offered my own parish which gave me great self confidence and a feeling of reward for the efforts I'd made not only in getting well again but in having given a pretty good service for eleven years in a community that deserved it and appreciated it.

I've no doubt, the Lord works in mysterious ways, because as I look back now, my stay in Kilcoole was extended by the authorities without me knowing it, simply to give me two to three years over and above, to fully recover from that last slip and prove that I was well enough and capable of taking on my own parish. If my departure had been any sooner, I probably would have been offered a parish at the other extreme of the diocese, way up the North East Coast. Now in hindsight what happened here and in many other departments of my life, was definitely providential. It so happened that by the time I was ready for the next phase in my ministry, a Parish very close to my home town, and an area I was quite familiar with, came on stream, and when it was offered to me I felt for sure that the Lord, despite all the physical and mental pain for me and all concerned, was in fact looking after me in a special way.

## *Esker-Lucan*
Being appointed to Esker-Lucan as Parish Priest, was my eighth and current appointment. It is very special, in that it is the culmination of a life-time of varied ministry. In earlier days thinking of becoming P.P. was a hope and a desire almost out of reach, but when it actually happened, I'm glad to say, it did not change me in attitude one bit as I thought it might. In the fifties and sixties, there was a sense of power still around, and unfortunately many clergy used, or should I say abused, their positions to capitalize on their status. That has changed so much today and I'm now very happy to be just a member of the team of three working in this lovely parish. The other two men are great to be with and although my predecessor remained in his house, again I was fortunate to acquire a very nice house in an estate quite near the church. I'm already into my third year, and together we have managed to make a few improvements, despite a third and definitive hiccup in my personal life. The on-going problem with the roof of the church has finally been resolved; the church has been carpeted and painted, outdoor floodlighting has been installed, and there are plans afoot for a parish office and some small meeting rooms to be built in the immediate future.

## CHAPTER NINE

## STRUGGLE WITH ALCOHOL

The subject of this chapter is quite difficult to speak about as it deals with private and intimate areas of my life. I'm going to try to be ruthless and thorough in my honesty. For many years I've been doing a lot of searching in vain for answers, when in fact I didn't even know the questions. I can only describe it as something going on within me in the deep subconscious, hammering at my brain and never really going away. In a variety of ways, this persistent yearning made its presence felt in the most basic departments of my life, physical, emotional, mental, spiritual and psychological. Either because I had ignored it or because I didn't know how to handle it, it demanded to be sorted out permanently. As I look back over the years, the old "Pleasing the people syndrome" became part of my every day life and endless activity was almost second nature to me. To a large extent this also controlled my method of praying. Very often the rattling of words which I thought were prayers, were in fact empty words which I can only describe as frantically blowing hot air into a balloon which had a gaping hole in it and getting nowhere, I'd quickly become exhausted. I called it babbling prayer. It took a lifetime of pain, hurt, anger, and frustration, to reach a point when I blocked out all this empty and fruitless activity, which was creating a sort of vacuum in my life. This left me wondering what all the effort was about, and that maybe I should try somehow to open the inner door of my feelings and searching, and let the Good Lord in, because He had been patiently waiting outside all this time, yes, waiting to be invited and allowed into my inner spiritually hungry being. For too long now I had felt like "The stone rejected by the builders," and longed for the day when I could feel I had become "The corner stone." (Acts 4:11)

Perhaps the human side of me was looking for a little love now and then, and whenever I was given some of that love, I always wished to give some back. Then I would realize the danger of seeking out an exclusive sort of love, and only end up hurting and being hurt. But for many years I was quite naïve in these matters and suffered a lot of misunderstanding at various times. People would often say to me, "Everybody loves you." While that's very nice to hear and I have for many years felt the real genuine love of many people, another part of me was yearning for some person or persons, who would love me for who I was, rather than, for what I was.

With those thoughts in mind, I look back on the drinking story of my life and the various stages that eventually led me into problems and all sorts of difficulties. Looking at the family background, my father drank a fair amount up to the time I was about nine or ten, but no one else in the house touched alcohol. In fact we all kept our Confirmation pledges and went on to be pioneers. Then I witnessed a dramatic promise from my father never to drink again when he himself was in his early fifties. So no member of the family took drink either at home or away. All the various socials and dances in those days were non-drinking events anyway. Even at the odd party we'd have at home, except occasionally, for some special visitor who might be given something, no family member ever indulged in any sort of alcohol. My mother would very rarely take a small sherry or such like and while some members of the family never drank for their entire lives, those who did, began quite late in life.

I was halfway through my London appointment when I took my first alcoholic drink, coming up to the age of thirty. It happened quite by accident when I visited some people one hot summer's afternoon and the humidity being high everyone needed something to avoid dehydration, and remarkably, the only liquid available in the house was wine. The water was off and there were no minerals or even milk. It seemed I had no choice and although strictly speaking, I was still a pioneer, I felt this was an emergency and should not really break the pledge. Unconsciously this was a kind of emancipation for me and shortly afterwards I began to explore many other kinds of alcoholic beverages. Soon I began and enjoyed some social drinking and as a result I justified this by saying it helped me meet with many people I wouldn't otherwise have met. It made going to the socials and clubs a lot easier and in fact I wondered why I hadn't done this long before then. I made inroads to a lot of places and people with the idea, "Well if you can't beat them join them," attitude. It opened up a whole new world to me and for the remainder of my time in London, I drank socially and it did not interfere with my life or work.

On returning to Rathcoole in 1972, I continued the same trend and never for one minute did I think that it would lead me to a problematic situation. During the latter period of my ten years there, I was conscious of overstepping my capacity on more and more occasions. But I still thought it was great to be one of the lads in the pubs and at various functions. Although the pattern was at that time beginning to affect my body and my work, at no stage during my time there did anybody refer to it, or suggest in anyway that there might be a problem. I myself certainly had not the remotest idea that an alcohol dependence syndrome in my genes was in fact beginning to surface and display its effects in more and more areas of my life. But I was told then by some of my brothers that both sets of grandparents, who we never knew, had serious alcohol problems in their lives.

Late in 1981, I moved to Navan Rd., and having continued a similar pattern of life for the first couple of years while settling in, I had no apparent problem. However, I did become worried and quite concerned when on many occasions I would need some drink first thing in the morning to settle me and get me started for the day. Although I was oblivious of the outward signs in my speech and of course the smell from my breath, people did begin to notice and talk about me secretly at first and then my own colleagues became aware and were genuinely concerned about me. Not only did I often need drink in the mornings, but I might also carry on during some days, and most nights. At night time, when I was out, I drank pints but during the late night hours or mornings, I would drink spirits. I did a lot of covering up, dodging, lying many times, denying blatantly, and even showing signs of aggression, which never had been part of my nature. Up to this period, the "few drinks" as I thought helped me to be the "life and soul of the party" but I didn't know what all this was really doing to me. I began to experience periods of depression and unhappiness. I would try to alleviate or ease the pain with yet another "few drinks." Then for the first time, the whole thing came to a head when I could cope no longer and found myself up against a stone wall. I was taken by my brothers to a treatment hospital and was told for the first time that I was an alcoholic. This was a devastating shock to me and I could not accept it at all. I went through the motions after being detoxed, of attending some after-care and promising to go to A.A. meetings. I did this for a couple of months and then thought I was okay, as long as I did not drink. I felt well and in fact did not drink for seven to eight years.

After moving down to Kilcoole, I continued in sobriety for some time and then foolishly thought, "Surely I should be able to take a little social drink again without running into difficulty." Little did I think that I was dealing with a very serious illness. I was to learn the hard way that it was a baffling, cunning and powerful, killer disease. One or all of these was affecting me without me knowing it. Only in a matter of months I was in trouble again. This time I started a different trend, i.e. doing a disappearing trick, into hotels in the hope that nobody would find me. I began to lose all sense of responsibility and any reckoning of time. My brothers and close friends would be frantically seeking my whereabouts, while I was in a different world and oblivious to their concern and deep worry. On one occasion a private detective was hired to try and find me. But I had my car very discreetly parked. More often than not, I would sign in under a false name and would not stay any longer than one night in any hotel. These were the bigger hotels in the city centre and as I paid in cash, it was difficult to trace me. So even the professionals failed to track me down. I knew nothing of all this until afterwards. During these disappearing escapades, I would have no intention of pulling myself together, simply because I was incapable of doing so, and I would have to be rescued and that was always achieved by my brothers. I did not realise how much pain, suffering and worry I had put them through. And so I ended up in the treatment centre again. This time it was a different one and I signed myself out on a couple of occasions, and once actually ran out of the place. I was given more than reasonable freedom to try and battle this on my own and no matter how hard I tried I would end up in what I can only describe as a "rat hole."

Even though I had gone five years this time without a real crisis, still it was a shorter period of sobriety, and once the drinking started, the "crash" came much quicker. Once again I found myself trapped in this awful hole with no way out and without help. I suppose putting it in my own way, I felt I'd become something like a time bomb, that only needed the slightest igniting to set it off, with even more serious and devastating consequences. I actually went to Lourdes with a group from Kilcoole, foolishly thinking I could handle it, and take a drink at the same time. I was only a couple of days there, when I cut myself off, disappearing to my hotel room and was not capable of performing my duties for the group I'd travelled with. These pilgrims of mine joined in with another Irish group and carried out all the usual ceremonies with them.

The people were very understanding and I'm so grateful, they never held it against me in anyway, but only wished to see me well. When there's support like that it gives one a great incentive to go and get things sorted out and return to normal. This subsequently was of great embarrassment. Word had got back, and I was met at the airport by my brothers, to be taken again to the original treatment centre. I literally hated being back there again and on this occasion the area bishop representing the diocese was brought in to monitor my progress. I did the six weeks again and went to some after-care; I also promised to attend A.A. I was frightened this time, especially when I realized for the first time that I had experienced some blackouts, in that I did not remember a lot of what had happened. Previously I thought blackout was actually fainting on the floor, but it's more to do with the memory being blocked and having no recollection of certain periods during the drinking session. I had sincere and very genuine intentions to make the very best of all that was being done for me. The support I had was great from family, parishioners, authorities, friends, and the professionals in the field of this illness. By giving me all the guidelines and direction needed to enable me remain sober, I could enjoy some real peace of mind, good health, satisfaction in work and basic happiness. I loved and enjoyed all that and realized I did not need alcohol for any of the reasons I used before. I remember being asked several times by people and in a special way by the first of my brothers to die, why did I drink. I honestly could not give an answer. If I could come up with a reason, a cause, a worry, an anxiety, a pressure, anything that could be looked at and resolved, this would be of some help. It was only when I really accepted the illness I had, that an in-depth searching was done and this showed a lot of frustration from early childhood and hang-ups concerning my own person, as the underlying reasons for my trying to find a solution in alcohol. I was so grateful for everything I had, my spiritual life and relationship with God were good and brought me great inner contentment. There were vibrant communities in all parishes where I worked, and I had a lovely home, car, money and all the accessories in life that I ever needed. What more did I want? I suppose I was stupidly trying to prove to myself and the world that somehow I could handle alcohol in a controlled manner. After all I'd done and had been told, I really thought I got the message and I was actually content and happy where I was in Kilcoole, and thrilled with the warm welcome home I got, I had no problem in staying on there indefinitely, and in fact deep down I didn't want to leave. Apart from great satisfaction in work and a feeling of good communication with God in all that I did, I thought I'd venture into an extra couple of sports areas. I took a decision to learn to fly a plane and I had instructions all lined up at the training centre just down the road. I took a trip up north with an adviser to look at some boats, about twenty footers on a trailer. So, thinking that the parish promotion would either be a long time in coming or perhaps never, I had these contingency plans as an occupational extra to make the best of the area I lived and worked in and so mentally prepared myself for further time where I was.

To my great surprise in May of 1997, the parish of Esker-Lucan was offered to me much sooner than I anticipated, and of course this gave me a terrific boost in self-confidence. I delved into the new and up lifting stage in my life with great enthusiasm and was thrilled to be so near home once again. With the retired man continuing to live in the area, two other lads on the team to help, a new house in a lovely estate, and wonderful people to work with, I could not ask for better. I now had a gem of a parish, and was simply delighted with myself.

About a year later in late November I was on a foreign holiday, and the cunning, baffling, powerful disease began to grapple at me again. I convinced myself, and with nobody to tell me otherwise, that a few beers would do me no harm and I'd be off it in time for Christmas and all would be well. The beer quickly advanced to spirits and I had a week of fear and bitter personal disappointment, not really enjoying it at all, being sick and unable to eat. I got home and with private medical help, managed to get off it and return to work. Christmas and New Year were good and I had no desire to take any sort of alcohol. Although my second eldest brother was quite ill, he was in no immediate danger and we were all assured of that. I felt in no way neglectful in taking my little after-Christmas break but once again the plan was in place to use the occasion to go back drinking. But before I even took myself away, I was already in the grips of the monster, not realizing that it was really only picking up where I'd started a month previous. The cunning aspect of the disease works on the mind in such a way that decisions can be made months in advance of going on a drinking spree. Plans would be put in place almost subconsciously, very deviously and without the individual even knowing what was happening, until it's too late. Anyway, against all advice, I took off and ended up in a foreign land again and instead of one week, it ran into three weeks. There was great anxiety at all levels at home without me knowing it. I had put myself in great danger. Many things were stolen from me, such as my phone, gold chain/cross and money. From a family inheritance I had some savings put aside but I squandered a substantial amount of it on this particular escapade. When I thought later of all the charitable things I could have done with the money, it made me feel very sad and guilty. I was later instructed by my counsellor to have my bank cards controlled by someone like a family member. At the time I very much resented this, as it further encroached on my freedom. But I realized when it was explained to me, that this was only in the event of me possibly running off again somewhere, that someone would have the power to pull the plug on my money. So I opened the way for this to be put in place.

I've no doubt that many people were praying for me, because how I ever got home, I'll never know. I had a bad experience at London Heathrow Airport with customs suspecting me of all sorts of things. Having been refused any further drinks on the flight, I couldn't wait to get to a bar on arrival. It appeared all was well as I passed through the green zone but a lady customs officer followed me and brought me back to the desk. I really must have looked a wreck, having had no food for three weeks, only drink. I was dirty in body and clothes and appeared like a mere tramp. She proceeded to go through everything in my suitcase and shoulder bag. I was asked to wait, and in the meantime I put my things back in the bag and suitcase. Just as I was finished she emerged again and went through the very same procedure. They must have suspected me of some wrong doing because of the state I was in. I was determined to keep cool and co-operate. This time every single item of paper and clothing was examined and questions asked regarding same. I was told to just sit and wait. With that an airport police customs officer appeared and he asked me to come along with him, and leave all my belongings just as they were. I entered into what appeared to be a detention room with heavy steel chairs and thick chains all over the floor. While I was not chained, he stood guard at the door in the meantime. The time was like an eternity and getting rather impatient, I asked the guard, how long this was going to take, and he said, "Until she's satisfied." This lasted two and a half hours. The lady officer, who was a plump, tough sort of cookie, arrived in with my two pieces of luggage very roughly repacked and told me I could go. As one of them opened a side door for me to exit into the main arrivals area, I merely said, "Thank you very much" in a very cynical manner, and the door slammed behind me.

I persuaded myself that I needed and deserved a drink immediately. But first I had to stock up on some sterling. I was literally fumbling, stumbling and shaking at the cash point, struggling to manipulate my bank card to extract some money. I was conscious of a bystander who was over anxious to help me. While I was suspicious, I was glad of the help, but did not realize at the time, that this guy was a professional con man. I invited him to join me for a drink, which he did. So while telling him of my ordeal and looking for sympathy and support as we delved into our drinks, I noticed I did not have my credit card. I asked him if he had seen it and accused him of taking it. With that he just got up from the table and disappeared quicker than a camera flash. I'd no doubt he had my card and my only worry was, whether he had seen me display my pin number. There was nothing I could do until I got to Dublin. I had the card cancelled and thank God there was no claim on the account. Then I wondered if I had enough money for the flight. But I had a second credit card and I hoped Aer Lingus would accept it, which they did. And so I was on a flight to Ireland. When I eventually got to Dublin Airport, I was trying desperately to get home, but my car which I'd left in the open, long-term parking area, had two flat and slashed tyres, and the battery was gone. There was no thought of making a call or getting a taxi. Nothing like that even entered my mind. All I was thinking of was where I was going to get another drink. I booked into a nearby hotel, thinking I'd get all I needed there, but there was no bar. So I left my luggage and went back to the airport bar, but it had closed for the night. At least I had a bed, but that was not what I wanted right then. I spent a restless night and was back around the airport trying to find an early bar, but with no luck. I then went and bought an air ticket to Manchester with no intentions of travelling, but with the boarding card, I could get into a departure lounge with a bar or perhaps into duty free. But admission there was not until after 9.30am. I half dozed off on a bench and noticed it was almost ten o'clock and I knew that in a half an hour all the bars would be open. I went back to try and have my ticket refunded, making some excuse about not travelling, but it was non-refundable. I tried to drink some minerals, as I was extremely thirsty (actually dehydrated) but I could not hold the container up to my mouth, so bad were the shakes. I went looking for my car again, but could not find it. I had to move from the hotel as the room was no longer available and on trying another one nearby, they said there might be a room, but they weren't sure. They allowed me to leave my bags and I spent the day around the airport mostly at the bars, until eventually a barmen refused to serve me having been instructed by the airport police. It was night time again, and having tried the hotel, there was no room, and I had to take my luggage which I hauled back to the main departure lounge. I was immediately confronted by the airport police who told me I was not welcome. I told them I'd no place to stay, and I asked if I could sleep on a bench, and they agreed. I decided to try upstairs for a quiet corner, carrying the heavy case and shoulder bag. I ascended the stairs as the escalator was stopped. I fell badly and got a deep cut in my shin. I had reached rock bottom and I knew I was beaten.

Before the end of that night the police had made contact with my family. I was brought to the airport police station and was picked up from there by my brothers. I was taken immediately to the treatment hospital, but they said I was in bad shape. Being so weak, I was taken by ambulance to a nearby general hospital as I had not eaten for three weeks, and was totally dehydrated. There was a long wait of several hours before I was admitted and during that time, I was totally aware of everything and I felt like shit. Three or four of my brothers stuck it out until I was actually in a bed. Up to this point I had expressed my sorrow over and over again and then during the long wait, I didn't say a word, just silently sat there and felt the depths of despair and guilt. I was on a drip for a week and returned to the treatment centre to start another six week programme. I had lost over two stone in weight, was totally shattered, physically, mentally, emotionally, and spiritually. I was a wreck and I knew it. For the first time I felt I had hit rock bottom and many people say that's often needed for some individuals to get the message. This time I was beaten, and when I was told there was damage to my liver and brain, I knew then I had put my life in real danger. I often heard of those with drink problems committing or contemplating suicide, and of the many drink related deaths that prove it's a killer disease. Here I was now on the same road, having brought myself quite close to death. In the meantime, my sick brother had deteriorated and was now dying. At the end of the second week back, I had just about enough strength to be taken to the hospital to see him, and he died the next morning. While I was somewhat consoled to have managed to get home to be there for his untimely departure, nonetheless, I was bitterly disappointed in myself, not to be able to play my proper role for his funeral and to support his wife and family at that time. I was going to have to live with this guilt and remorse over the weeks and months to come.

Following a six week programme and intensive treatment, a very difficult meeting in the presence of doctor, counsellor, family and the area bishop, took place, and, I was made feel as low as is possible for a human being. I was stripped of everything and I was told that I must go somewhere for three or possibly six months on a recovery programme. Not only was I bombarded from all corners, which I took in complete silence, but I was told to resign my parish and to have no further association with "The Priests Show." The consultant also stated in the presence of the same company that he had grave reservations about me resuming ministry again. All members of my family stated that they would be willing to accept my leaving if it came to that, either by choice or direction. But that was an option I never seriously considered and even at that very vulnerable stage of the proceedings, I was quietly building a determination in my mind not to allow this awful plight in which I found myself, to dictate to me what my life and future were to be. I was going to make every effort to get well again in order to make the choice myself. I cried bitterly all of that day and night and pleaded on my outstretched body on the floor to the Good Lord to help me. The thought of signing myself out and clearing off crossed my mind but where was that going to get me. Surely I'd drink again and certainly end up dead. The two choices were summed up by words from the letters of the word FEAR :- Feck Everything And Run; or: Face Everything And Recover. I had tried the former option many times and ended up in the rat hole of despair. I chose the latter and very sensible one and I'm so glad I did. It was not easy and I had to do it on my own. West Cork was the venue agreed for this extended recovery programme and I drove the five hour journey on the Bank Holiday, Easter Monday morning, April $5^{th}$ 1999. I realized that it was my birthday, and thinking to myself that the only possessions I had were the car I was driving and the clothes on my back. Some of the professional people who had taken me through treatment, thought I would not reach my destination without stopping at a pub. That's how much confidence they had in me. I did stop at a pub, but it was for a coffee. One of my more thoughtful brothers called me on the mobile and wished me well. This was an extremely lonely and sad journey for me and the thought of living in community in a religious house, certainly did not appeal to me. It was late afternoon of that day when I reached my final destination, called Myross Wood. The driveway was a mile long into a lovely wooded estate of one hundred and thirty acres of trees, rock and rolling hilly land. The original old house had been restored and extended into a retreat centre run by eight priests, one of whom was to be a personal counsellor to me while there. I was advised to attend at least three A.A. meetings per week and to travel every Friday to Kinsale, which was about an hour away to an after-care group. I decided to give this my best shot or die. And so began for me what they call in this particular programme, "Life's Healing Journey". The community was friendly and welcoming and made, what was for me a desperate uphill struggle, somewhat lighter and encouraging. It was down to work straight away by putting in place the plan for this journey of healing. Each morning I met my counsellor for about an hour and while he outlined his plan for me, he insisted that the success or failure of this whole exercise depended on myself, and no one was going to be checking me, monitoring progress, or interfering. I preferred it that way. A pattern was soon established, with a morning session, some writing and reflecting, plenty of walking was vital, gardening and a little farming. There were numerous A.A. meetings around the general area and I adopted one or two as regulars and I travelled every Friday to Kinsale for the after-care. Putting all of this together was an opportunity I'd never had before, because I'd never taken a sabbatical in my career. I was not going to get this chance again and this realization made me all the more determined not to falter.

I remember thinking to myself that with all the travelling, experiences, ups and downs of the growing and learning in my life to this stage, that surely I should have reached a certain level of capability to understand and cope with any situation in the world, but most especially in my own life. But I was stripped to the core and had to face the most fundamental questions of who and what I was, and what I wished to be, for the rest of my life. If ever I felt like the character of the "footsteps in the sand" story, I did at this point. But I knew I had to rely on the Faith which thank God was not gone altogether, only weakened. During my drinking sprees, all responsibilities towards work, God, prayer life, family and friends, were disregarded. So the God who always meant so much to me was during this period virtually non-existent. So it was time to start building bricks. Paradoxically, each time I had one of these slips, it was always at a time when everything was fine and I was in good form with no apparent problems. I felt in full control. But suddenly all that disappeared whenever I started drinking again. The cunning disease conned me into a false sense of security, in making me think I could handle some little alcohol because of a certain situation. My main desire was to get back up there, find myself, God, people and regain that confidence to be once again, "top of the walk."

So treatment progressed to recovery and there's a huge difference. The journey in all its three aspects of counselling, after-care, and A.A. was a very spiritual one and I was amazed when I began to hear stories of people who had abandoned God or maybe never believed in Him, talking about their Higher Power and recognizing Him under that heading as their only way back to sobriety. I had a real challenge on my hands, coupled with the fear of having to let go. For the first time in my life in all areas as mentioned above, I made a sincere and genuine effort to put God at the centre. It was like learning how to walk, swim, or ice skate. My natural determination played a major role here and I first had to wind down, try to be calm, quiet, and let what was now being offered to me, slowly but surely have its effect on me.

The early part of the counselling involved probing into my whole upbringing and background, trying to discover what was going on in the subconscious. God came up under a variety of headings, No God; Ideal God; Testing God; Philosophical God; Santa Clause God. As a believer in a true and personal God, I began to understand that suffering is a mystery to be lived, not to be solved. For so long I had been advising other people in their lives without ever focusing on my own. While my message over the years to my listeners was sincere I felt myself somehow on the outside of what I was saying. I always liked making decisions, and to think that others depended on me to a certain extent. In the early stages of recovery, "the letting go" demand, was giving me real problems. While I was there physically and in person, and verbally stated I'd let go, and also wrote letters of resignation of my parish and of the priests show, mentally and emotionally I realized I had a lot to do. I began to really listen at the A.A. meetings and took away some word or phrase every time to ponder while driving back to base. The same words and phrases kept cropping up like: acceptance....letting go.... hand it all over to the higher power....things will get better....this too shall pass...easy does it....de-nial is not a river in Egypt ..........let go, let God.....one day at a time. Of course the serenity prayer summed it all up, "God grant me the serenity to accept the

things I cannot change, the courage to change the things I can, and the wisdom to know the difference."
Part of the programme involved what was called "The Enneagram" which is a study of various types of personalities. This outlined the traits of my own personality both negative and positive, which in turn was a great help in figuring out some of the areas in my life that presented problems. The realization that only an estimated 12% of our knowledge is in our conscious awareness while the other 88% is in our unconscious awareness really amazed me. This went a long way towards explaining some of the underlying reasons for me to be seeking answers in alcohol which only added to the problem. I soon discovered that there were many areas in my life which I never really confronted with professional direction and guidance. Anger had built up which I could trace back to childhood relating to parents, to my lot in life and to the choices I made. There was a lot of hurt in my life. It took little to make me feel guilty, especially after a drinking binge. The area of sexuality, had to be addressed and properly understood, as that too showed great immaturity in me while on a spree. Looking back on my journey in life to this point, I honestly tried so hard for years to do as much as I could for others, and I could not say "no" to anyone. I always thought that to do something for oneself was selfish and self-centred, and for the very first time I was hearing loud and clear, "You've got to do all of this for yourself." All of the things that were obviously creating difficulties in my life- anger, guilt, shame, remorse etc. - had to be sorted out once and for all. The only way to do that, I began to realize, was to accept the stripping served up to me and leave a clear and uncomplicated path focused only on my personal recovery. I sought guidance and prayed daily in these words, "Lord reveal to me what you want to heal in me."
The scripture stories of the prodigal son and the grain of seed falling to the ground and dying, became very relevant to me. The first time I shared in group and at A.A. was a breakthrough. I can only describe it as bursting a hole in a

wall and beginning to see light on the other side. I had never shared at anything anywhere before, in fact I could never see the point in any of their methods. I realized to myself that I had never got anything from these groups or meetings, because I had never put anything into them. To state in public that, "I am an alcoholic," as I began to do and never thought I would, gave a true sense of freedom and inner relief that can only be experienced by the one who does it. For the first time I saw hope emerging, and that somehow I was going to make it. For so long I'd been told that things would get better and they did. My goal in setting out on my journey to West Cork was to get back all that was taken from me as soon as possible, and maybe even shorten my stay down there. This soon changed as I became involved in the real significance of the course and the one and the most important aim for me was to get well, gain sobriety in all its fullness and develop it into a better quality of life. I had to change. Things were never going to be the same again. The healing was in the letting go. From "Life's Healing Journey,"(compiled by the Sacred Heart Fathers, Myross Wood). I digested certain phrases not to be forgotten. "Until the pain of what I have is greater than the fear of what change might do to me, I will never let go." And again as I was hoping not to lose heart when obvious progress was being made, I will never forget the dramatic quote, "On the sands of hesitation bleach the bones of those, who close to victory, stopped to rest and in resting, died."

People ask if I will ever drink again, I always say no. I've said that several times before and we all know what happened. But this third major crisis was no doubt the worst and most frightening of all my drinking experiences and when told that I nearly killed myself, or at least caused possible permanent damage, I realize now that my very life was on the line. I'm now saying to myself, not so much that I won't drink again, but rather that I can't drink again.

Having done a little study in child psychology some years ago, I found the section of this journey where we explored the whole area of healing the child within us and self-parenting, most interesting and meaningful. I grew up with very low self-esteem and only at this stage was I really coming to terms with the reality that I am somebody who loves and can be loved. I started at the very bottom again and stripped myself to my very roots to start building my life more or less from the beginning. "Allow yourself to visualize a world where you are loved and love others," from *"A Spirituality in Love of Brokeness,"* by Eilis Bergin. And from the same, "We need to realize that replacing fear with faith is the beginning of letting go of the past and finding our real recovery from the traumas of our childhood." "I replace fear with faith and turn my personal darkness into light." I never thought that by allowing acceptance rule my attitude with regard to the illness, there would be such a big difference. When I first began this course I hated everybody associated with sending me there, but now in hindsight, how right they were. It has turned my whole life around. I was not afraid any more and during my eventual interview with the powers that be, to decide whether I was to resume ministry or not, I was totally at ease with whatever the outcome was to be. I was prepared to fully accept the ruling of this meeting and I was most pleasantly surprised to be told that after a month's holiday I could return to my parish. I remembered the words of Trina Paulus in *"Hope for the Flowers"*, from the study of caterpillars and metamorphosis, changing into butterflies. "What's really you will still live, life is changed, not taken away. Change does not mean to lose but to have all that's possible."

Just the same as fear spoke a message so did, AWARE: Able, Willing And Ready to Exchange. I had learned the true meaning of the word forgiveness towards myself and others; yes that forgiveness creates a sense of change as it is a choice and not a feeling. I also learned to talk and open up on so many issues in my life that were never really addressed before. While sharing at an A.A. or group meeting, I tended to speak briefly but I found that putting things on paper in writing or typing, had a great therapeutic effect. Sometimes it's good to write about an anger or guilt concerning someone or some thing, and then tear it up later. It's a real means of getting rid of it, or burying it. Being quiet and still, never came easy to me, but I learned to do that also. It took a lot of effort and practice, but I was told if you keep trying, things will get better, and they did. From *"Opening Doors Within"* by Eileen Caddy, I read, "When you can accept that I am within you, never again will you feel alone; never again will you have to search without for the answer to your problems. But when anything arises which needs answering, you will seek that peace and stillness within, lay your questions and problems before Me, and I will give you the answers." The Lord speaks in these words.

I was re-assured by my counsellor that in his opinion I should definitely stay in ministry and that made me very happy. One morning at Mass in the oratory at Myross Wood, where my course was now nearing completion, a young man had just finished his retreat before his ordination and everybody was wishing him well, as I did myself. There was a mixed group of priests, nuns, brothers, and lay people on this particular journey of which I was part. This young man's forthcoming ordination brought the memory of my own back very vividly and I felt, how I would have loved to be going for ordination myself with the knowledge and maturity and understanding I had right then. But that was only trying to go back in time. So I asked before leaving if a little ceremony for renewal of vows could be arranged for priests and those professed who were present. The priest in charge agreed to do this and everybody with vows took the opportunity to renew theirs also. This was arranged and I must say, that had much more meaning for me that my original ordination day itself.

### *After thoughts and feelings*
It was with thoughts of gratitude and a sense of achievement, that I concluded my four months, including a holiday, and as I

made my way to my home, parish, family and friends, it was with a prayer of "Life's Healing Journey" by the Missionaries of the Sacred Heart, on my lips and in my heart: "How I wish You would enter my life, brighten my path with the light of Your Presence. My anger, my sadness, my pain are all around me like a high wall. But like the prophet in the mid-fire stream, shall I walk unharmed with you—by my side an inner strength, sustains and encourages me, so that barriers and walls fade away like paper in fire." The outstanding message and uppermost thought on my mind, was that of forgiveness, first towards myself, as that's where it begins, and then to seek it from all those near and dear to me, whom I may have hurt in anyway. It is one of the steps in AA to seek a mutual forgiveness where possible and whether people move with it or not, that's their priority. I had a plan now firmly fixed in place to tackle a new and changed approach to myself, to people, to God, to family, and friends. I was in an upbeat mood to move on and as I'd buried the past and all that went with it, the only way was forward. I hoped and prayed that this time I got it right, having put so much really hard work into the journey and handing it over eventually to God, knowing that by doing so, things would get better which they eventually did.

Naturally, I had apprehensions about a lot of things, like getting back into routine work, facing my parishioners once again and explaining my situation plainly and honestly, hoping I'd be able to keep up all the promises and resolutions I'd made and so on. I felt I'd changed, therefore things were going to be different and I would have to make certain things change. My spiritual life was going to need constant and daily attention, and for that reason, I decided to make a little prayer room in my house, which is now in place and which I find great. I read and pray much more each day than I ever did before. My social life needed attention and change. Life without "The Priests Show" would obviously leave a gap and I had decided that the time devoted to that over the years, would now be re-directed into better liturgies, and more church-related activities. I have to mention that at no time during the many years I spent with the show from its very foundation, was there ever a query that the life style associated with that business, had anything to do with my drinking problem. If the reason had been anywhere in that department, I would have left it, or would have been told to leave it, long ago. The reason I was asked to resign after this final and serious slip, was that to be in recovery and at the same time appearing to have a high profile on stage and at shows, did not seem to be in the proper spirit of what I was endeavoring to do. Naturally I was going to miss it and all the friends I made over the years, but I had to get my priorities right and so my recovery and ministry were my primary concern. I'm very grateful for all the benefits I reaped from the show in the area of experience, travel, and friendship.

Shortly after returning, a layman friend of mine, told me how he too was at the early stages of recovery and finding it difficult. He explained how some people don't really understand what it's all about. He told me how for many years he went to a neighbour's house for a New Year's party, and this year was special being the millennium. He accepted the fact that he was an alcoholic, but he worried about how was he going to explain this to all his friends. He wondered whether or not he should go to the party or just forget it altogether. After long deliberation, he decided he'd go, grab the nettle and tell his friend and all present of his illness. He knocked on the door and the host himself answered with open armed welcome, but before taking one step in the door, the rather nervous guest spoke. "Listen, before I go I in I want you to know something, I'm an alcoholic." The rather happy and already "in the party mood" host answered, "That's no problem, come right in, we have plenty of booze in the house." Talk about missing the point!

Having had plenty of time to think and now begin to plan ahead, I thought to myself how very lucky and blest I was, that there was no incident hanging over me, like a road accident with someone hurt or killed, no legal proceedings of any sort in the pipe line, no serious or permanent damage to my own health. However I realized that family members, friends, parishioners, superiors, colleagues, may have felt hurt and let down and I don't blame them one bit. I knew I had ground to repair, hills to level, and roads to straighten, but in time, all that too would pass. The most important thing on my mind was huge gratitude for being well and in control, and I was determined no matter what happened, not to let anyone or anything take that from me. Without drink nothing in life that came my way was any problem, whereas with drink, everything was a problem. I decided on my return to the parish to speak at all the Masses and put my cards on the table, so as not to leave any misunderstanding out there with the people. I thought carefully about what to say and as I seldom or ever write or use any notes if at all possible, so I hoped I could do this in the same fashion without omitting any important details. There was no reference book I could consult as a guideline, because such a book had not been written. This was my story, my circumstances, my responsibility, and so nobody but myself could express the real truth. I knew the whole day was going to be difficult and draining, both physically and mentally. Anyway I really wanted to do this, because I had the gut feeling it was the thing to do and I felt it would clear the air, leave no misunderstandings, and most of all, I felt I owed it to the people. As to how they were going to react, I had no idea.

Because I spoke without notes I have no written record of what I actually said, and from memory I can say that it did open with an apology for my long absence of nearly five months and then went on straight away to explain that I had been informed by doctors that I had an alcohol dependence syndrome and that anything with an alcohol content would be detrimental to all areas of my health and life. In other words I had an illness called alcoholism, but now that it's arrested and treated and I continue my life in total sobriety, then there is no reason why I can't carry on a normal life and work. I admitted to being a person who was vulnerable, dependent, willing to accept help and had no problem in living with that reality. I explained how the disease was powerful, cunning, and baffling and in my recent relapse, I had crashed out into a very bad state of health of mind and body. I compared it to a serious road accident, where those involved would be dependent on all the services to rescue the injured, that it happened suddenly and totally unexpectedly. I went on to thank all those who helped along the way, family, friends, doctors, counsellors, superiors, local fellow priests, classmates, colleagues, and I complimented the parishioners on their kindness in sending cards, and support messages. Without all of this I could not have survived. The One I wish to thank most of all I left to the end, because He's the most important, i.e. God. Without Him the journey back would not have been possible, and so I owe Him an eternal debt of gratitude. I vowed to work with and for the parish as best I could and that I saw a great future together. I spoke for about eight to ten minutes and finished with the serenity prayer, "God grant me the serenity to accept the things I cannot change, the courage to change the things I can and the wisdom to know the difference." To my great surprise I got a huge applause and at several of the Masses this included a standing ovation. I was overcome with such a positive reaction and it affirmed me in what I'd said and an appreciation of the courage shown to take this line of return. I was simply delighted with the welcome and the encouragement received, apart from the many requests for help which also resulted.

While this got me off to a great start and I was able to settle into normal life and work fairly quickly, I felt a great ease and relaxed approach to whatever came my way. The thing that bothered me most at this point was not being capable of playing my role properly on the occasion of my brother's death and being there for his family. I was so down and ill at the time. His death left an effect on me I will always remember, but I had a little consolation at least, that I was there, and perhaps it would have been a lot worse both for me and the family if I had not arrived back in time. I did my grieving for him while I was away in West Cork and one of the first things I did after returning was to visit his grave, pray for him and to him, asking him to help me through all of this. I wrote a long apologetic letter to all members of his family and visited them as soon as I could. Their warmth, reception and understanding made me very happy and I promised to try and be a father figure to them when in need. I've no doubt the Good Lord was working through all of this.

Experiencing the first of my immediate family to die was in a way very similar to losing the first parent many years previous. Being a large family I thought to myself that we'd been quite fortunate that no father or mother of the second generation was taken when their families were young and needy. The faith within all the extended family members, was very strong and really shone out for me at this brother's funeral, because instead of being up there on the altar doing the ceremony, I was with them in the pews, and in a sense I felt the hand of the Lord working again for me, because I was in a way actually supportive of them, being there.

I compared myself to the story of the man giving a wedding feast and his invited guests refused to come, whereupon he ordered people of all sorts to be brought in from the highways and byways to fill up his wedding banquet. (Luke 14.) I could identify with those down-and-outs in having the feeling of transformation from outcast to one of respectability especially in God's eyes. There was here a sense of handing over to His power because I was going nowhere without Him, only to death in body and spirit.

# CHAPTER TEN

## BEREAVEMENTS

As I am writing this (April 2000), I realize that the week-end which is upon us, is just about the anniversary of my journey to West-Cork. If any person was to say to me at this point in time one year ago, that in addition to the death of my second eldest brother, whom I had just lost, that his wife and two other brothers would also be dead and buried, within a year, I would have told them they were crazy. Neither would I have believed that I'd be well on the way to writing my life and experiences in a book form. Yet all this is true. I'm no expert on the subject of bereavement, but I can tell what it feels like to experience the loss of family members in such quick succession. All through the years it was part of my ministry, supporting and being with families during their periods of bereavement, and I can safely say, my colleagues also agree, that I have not come across a family to have lost so many in less than a year. Mature and experienced people could only offer expressions of sympathy in words like, "I just don't know what to say."

Just as we were beginning to recover from the first death of the second generation, that was in February 1999, I got a phone call to my hotel in Lourdes where I was with a group from Esker-Lucan, to say that my eldest brother was seriously ill. I cut my stay short and made my way back and went straight to the Hospital, where he died a week later. (September 1999).

About six weeks later, we were again just getting back on our feet, and I had agreed to join some family members on a one week break. My third eldest brother phoned me the night before departure to wish us well. That was at 9.30pm and I had a phone call at 10.15pm that same night to say he was dead. This was a huge shock to all as it came totally out of the blue. (October 1999).

It was towards the latter part of January 2000 that I met some colleagues for lunch in the city and just before starting I had a phone call to say, my sister-in-law, the wife of the first brother to die, was herself, dead.

This run of events was unbelievable and very difficult to understand, and as they all occurred close to a planned trip by me, I now have no inclination or desire to plan any more trips for the foreseeable future. I've no doubt but for the faith that was very much part of the entire family, we could not have survived. Apart from the first one, I was most grateful to the Lord to be well and able to play my role fully at the funerals and towards the families. Even though we were a large family, nobody expected so many to die in such quick succession. Through it all, I never heard one word of complaint against God and His plan, and that for me was something to be very proud of and gave me great courage to present the liturgies for the funerals.

Grieving is something that every individual must live and cope with themselves. You don't learn the "how" from books or the experience from others, one can only take it step by step, and it's the same for young and old alike. After the trauma and crowded scenes of each death and funeral, life quickly returns to normal for those on the outer circle, but for close blood and marriage relatives, it's a slow and very often painful experience and while they have the support of the immediate family, no one can do the grieving for them. To use a metaphor, it is like the loss of a limb. While the person concerned cannot obviously forget or deny the absence of the limb, they can nonetheless learn to live without that part of their body and to manage somehow to compliment the loss by doing extra with what's left to the now incomplete body. It is natural when one loses an arm, that the other one becomes twice as strong, and likewise with a leg, or an eye or ear. The struggle is slow and painful at the beginning but the human being is very resourceful and will always in time find a way of coping. When the person has faith and trust in God, then that is a great help and support. Only He knows the reason behind all this, and in the long run, trust and faith in Him, will be rewarded. It's a very interesting fact that immediately following on these deaths, four new children arrived to the next generation, to replace the four just gone. It's almost like the balance of nature in action. We are part of all this folding and unfolding which brings death and new life. As changes are right now very much part of my personal life, I am also part of the changes taking place in the extended family. I feel, like everyone else, I've got to go along with it. So in faith I feel a willingness to change where and when necessary, and I'm again so grateful for the confidence and faith to go with it.

Within such a large family as ours, drifting among the more extended members is part of life, but these recent happenings, have brought everybody together like never before. "We should not wait for someone to die to come together," one niece said to me. Any little differences that may have existed between some relations, were quickly overlooked and forgotten, as all were in unison during the grieving periods. Personally I always advise and recently had to exercise, a positive and perhaps even optimistic, approach when struggling through the more difficult periods. But I did feel very much like a member of a team physically huddled together to re-group for the next phase in life and that in itself gave a great sense of unity, solidarity, friendship and support. People from outside the immediate family, were and always are of great solace and consolation to grieving families.

In ministry, I would have been with so many families in many places and in a wide variety of circumstances. One learns from all this. But until the first death in our immediate family in 1977, i.e. of my father, only then did I learn the real meaning of pain and loss. The hurt inside and what the future holds without this member, including dependence on Christian beliefs, are all part of the personal experience. When people express the traditional phrase, "I'm sorry for your troubles," and many such commonly used phrases, while they mean well and are sometimes even "sorry with" the bereaved, very often it can be a mere exercise in duty and might be no deeper than that. But until one can be inside the heart of the person grieving, it is impossible to understand. Still, "a presence" is all important and remembered by all concerned. Sometimes people's absence is noted and feelings of disappointment are expressed subsequently. In the exercise of ministry on these occasions, again the bodily presence of the priest, in the home, at the funeral, by the grave side, the follow-up support, are all remembered and appreciated. I learned recently that the funeral of elderly retired priests can be a sad and lonely event, because often they have no family as such alive. A colleague came into the sacristy recently having attended such a funeral and he said to the company, "Nobody cries at a priest's funeral," and "There's nothing so dead as a dead priest." In my own experience of many sad and tragic circumstances, while I would have really felt sorry for those bereaved and would have given generously of time and support, I was nonetheless like many others very much an outsider, doing a job and fulfilling a ministry. I would have left a lot to God and His role, making His Presence known and felt at the crucial period by the sacramental ministry of the priest.

I was asked in recent months, many times, what it was like up there at the family funeral ceremonies so many times, in such quick succession. I can honestly say I felt a sense of gratitude and appreciation and I felt honoured at being there in my role. Also of course I felt hurt and pain. I did my share of crying for the deceased, I visited the grave sides many times and on occasions late at night when all the flickering night lights gave a sense of life somewhere else, I was alone while other members had their own families. When it came to performing the liturgy in the presence of bishops and fellow clergy, of so many people and close friends, somehow my whole system went into an appropriate "mode" suited and geared for what was required of me at the time. I can only thank God for that. He gave me some special strength to hold up and do what I had to do, for the deceased, the family and all present. Many people admire it as a gift or a talent in me, and if that's so, I've only the Lord to thank for that gift and strength which He gave me when needed most.

My struggle with alcoholism over the years and my present state of sobriety which I treasure and will fight to maintain, coupled with all the family bereavements, make me humbly feel like the saintly Dublin man, Matt Talbot. I, like him, found the way back to God through alcoholism and bereavement. I can identify with the words written on a piece of paper found in his pocket after he died, "God so loved the world that He gave His only Son so that all who believe in Him, may not be lost, but may have eternal life."

## CHAPTER ELEVEN

## THE CHURCH
### *YESTERDAY-TODAY-TOMORROW*

My memory of church during my childhood is, I'm sorry to say, not a very happy one. Like all families of that era, we were no different, and what the parents of the day lived and handed on to us was accepted without question. When it came to the subject of God, Church, Religion, praying, an air of awe was immediately created, and in a sense nothing else was important at that time. Whatever the Pope, bishops, or priests said, was gospel and therefore could not be wrong. Whenever a priest came to our house, he was given total and undivided attention, and over the years I can recall some of these priests taking advantage of their situation. I can remember even then having a gut feeling that something was wrong here but I couldn't do anything about it, nobody could. The combination of church and state was all-powerful and there were no alternatives, no freedom, complete smothering and saturation. I also had the feeling that this way of life could not last forever, and in the 50's as the republican free state of the South of Ireland was really making its presence felt, and the aftermath of the second world war was fading into history, the close-knit relationship of church and state were beginning to drift apart somewhat.
But the church is like life itself, she's a survivor, and can be compared very much to life when the writer Robert Byrne, speaks of life in the first person, "I have been misused

throughout centuries through war, poverty, rebellion, revolt and famine. Above all I have been abused by people from within their own lives through pride, covetousness, lust, envy, gluttony, anger and sloth. I speak of faith, hope, charity, justice." From my earliest days, I vowed to try at least within my own jurisdiction through ministry, (if I made it that far) to do my bit at least in creating an atmosphere that Christ is with and in the church through the ministry of her priests, religious and people. I suppose the little revolt going on within me was that if I were to be a priest, that I did not wish to be like many of the ones I'd already met. Not saying they were all the same; some were very kind and likable, it was only the few as usual who gave the wrong impression. In these minority of cases, often common courtesy would be lacking and that's all it would have taken to bring a Christ-like attitude into church by her ministers. In the words of Francis Gay from "The Friendship Book," "Courtesy is like the air in tyres-it doesn't cost anything, but it makes travel a lot more comfortable."

Looking back at the church as it appeared to me in the years of education and early ministry, the heavy impression of POWER and INFALLIBILITY struck me very forcibly. While it was true that the church did a great deal for people and country in setting up centres of education and social welfare which left its mark to this very day, nevertheless, there was a separatism which also left its mark. Latin was still the official language used at Mass and all church ceremonies, and so as the ordinary people of the country were still struggling from lack of education, lack of opportunities, social and economic deprivation, this "Latinism" and air of superiority created an even greater gulf between church and people. It is easy I suppose to be critical when looking back from our present standpoint, but still credit must be given to the church bodies of those days for the amount of support and direction they gave to people. There was nothing else available and it was an accepted fact that people often turned to the priest, doctor, lawyer, school teacher for their educated assistance in many aspects of every-day life. I'm grateful to have grown up, lived, and later worked in and through that system, because it enabled me to see both sides of past and present from actual experience.

All that was to change dramatically for a number of reasons. People in all three levels of education were asking very fundamental questions on what was being offered by the church. A process of negativity through materialism and secularization was setting in. Young enthusiasts on radio and television programmes make no mention of religion. The superstitious and tribal follow-on mentality no longer exist, as people are now thinking for themselves. A crisis now exists not just in Ireland but right across Western and Eastern Europe, emerging from historical, social and economic reasons. The many scandals that were revealed and brought to light and to justice, contributed greatly to the crisis, and created a reality that church authorities and faithful never thought existed, but had no choice in the matter except to face the consequences and work through a process of cleansing and growth. The question constantly asked is whether the rule of celibacy is a contributory factor in the falling of vocations? Maybe, but contributory only, and I feel we're looking here at a crisis of faith and not just one factor only. For me celibacy is an on-going personal battle but I'm aware that is what I took on from the very beginning. I have no problem with the idea of a married clergy and all through my priestly life, I had a very traditional outlook on this matter. For many years until recently it would have been one or the other. I could never see myself possibly having two roles to fulfil and felt I could not divide myself between God and a committed family life. In recent years I've had a change of heart and not only do I accept the compatibility of a married clergy in the Catholic Church and that this would be fully acceptable to the faithful in general, but I believe in addition that it will come if not in this generation, then certainly in the next.

The faith and stamina of all believing Christians are being very much put to the test today and in a society of the "celtic tiger" leaders, religious and lay are suffering low morale but not without hope for the future. People feel the fall-off in attendance at church will continue to a lower ebb, and even if that were so, I would not be discouraged one bit. Let us nourish and foster what we have and branch out from there.

I digress slightly for a moment to tell you a story of three priests in the U.S. who were in neighbouring parishes but all three had a common problem with their buildings, the ceilings were infested with bats. After trying just about everything without success, one of them eventually shared his solution which worked. I found the answer he said, "I baptized and confirmed them, and I never caught a sight of them afterwards."

While the seminaries throughout the country are all virtually empty, the hope for the future of the church in my opinion lies fair and square in the hands of the laity. The colleges and seminaries are now developing a practical networking of priests and people. These centres are being used for study courses. An interactive process, not academic, simple courses are being devised for ordinary people to follow and understand; a learning process that will give people a true understanding of mission within the Christian community, and they can stand up and say, "I AM THE CHURCH." While there is great talent and potential among the people of any parish or community, sometimes those who respond to the offer of courses for a missionary people, could unfortunately be the usual few reliable ones: a) those sent by the priest; b) the "charismatic" type; c) those who go to courses anyway. Therein lies a danger and it would be much better to look at a broader and all- inclusive approach for the new and better structured future for the church in giving the people as a whole a true sense of mission as their role in the Christian Community.

I personally am optimistic and with God's help will never lose heart. Lots of suggestions are being tossed around, especially when the Church in Ireland is viewed at least from a European viewpoint. With the shortage of actual priests on the ground, re-distribution of priests and re-grouping of parishes is something that's happening in many parts of Europe. While the idea of ministry at the Deaconate level is growing and strongly suggested, I don't for one moment accept that as the solution. Lay involvement is a must and in my opinion is the future of the church. It's the only real and obvious option left open, before it's too late entirely. The Tridentine style seminary will cease as it's in terminal decline and I think the way forward is to call people to ministry, to prepare them for ministry. This could be a gradual process working at different age levels. A living parish community could create an apprenticeship model of calling to create an atmosphere conducive to some people perhaps going into special ministry. There could be a period then of transition possibly into the priestly ministry. There is no doubt a different kind of priest is needed today and I would like to think that what I do and live and try to create within the Christian Family is relevant, supportive and uplifting, as evidence of Christ's Presence amongst us.